George Adamski

When a Philosopher has passed a certain number of years for the upliftment of humanity, having fulfilled the purpose of his soul upon incarnation, he earns the right to retire from the world and to enjoy the freedom demanded for his own spiritual evolution. In the Order of the Philosophers are enrolled the names of many Brothers who have feigned death.

Perhaps he merely pretended to die, as is the way of Philosophers, who feign death in one place, only to transplant themselves to another.

---The Abbe N. de Montfaucon de Vilars

Gray Barker's

BOOK OF ADAMSKI

ILLUSTRATED

Cover Illustration by Gene Duplantier
Photographs Courtesy August C. Roberts,
Joseph L. Ferriere and Michael G. Mann

We wish to thank the many others who
contributed so generously of their
time, ideas and talents to help make
this book possible.
                                      The Publisher

Copyright © 2014 by: New Saucerian Books
Pt. Pleasant, WV

ISBN: 1-4991-0511-8
ISBN-13: 9781499105117

CONTENTS

GO IN PEACE! 9
Desmond Leslie
Alice K. Wells

THE GREATEST SAUCER STORY EVER TOLD 13
Gray Barker

"ADAMSKI'S PHOTOS ARE REAL" 23
Michael G. Mann

MY FIGHT WITH THE SILENCE GROUP 33
George Adamski

QUESTIONS AND ANSWERS 39
George Adamski

SPACE AGE PHILOSOPHY 49
George Adamski

MOON PROBES CONFIRM ADAMSKI'S CLAIMS 57

THE STRANGE CASE OF R. E. STRAITH 61
Gray Barker

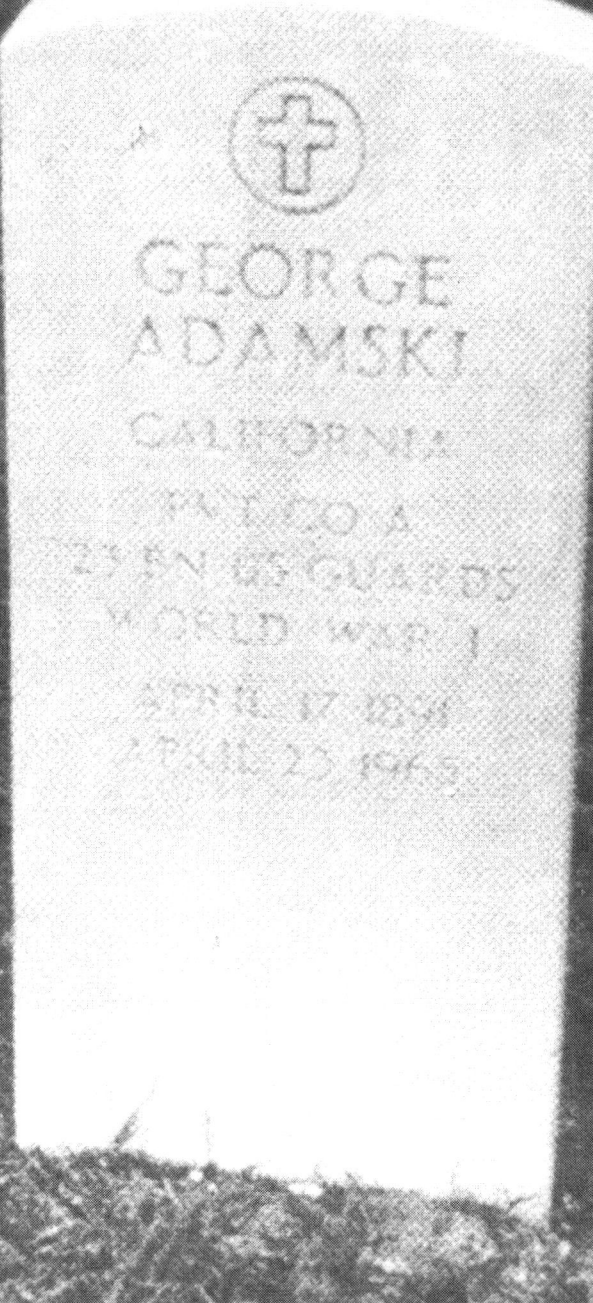

"The more I know Adamski, the more convinced I become that he must either be accepted in toto or completely rejected."

-----Desmond Leslie

Go In Peace!

Desmond Leslie
Alice K. Wells

June 1965

On the evening of April 23, 1965, a call came from Silver Springs, Maryland, that George Adamski had been rushed to the hospital with a heart attack, that I would be called as soon as his condition was determined. The call came and the Doctor said they had given him every emergency treatment but he did not respond and he was gone. This did not come as a complete shock to me for I had been forewarned that this might happen and George Adamski had told me exactly how he wanted his body cared for after he no longer had use for it.

On the morning of April 24th, I flew back to Washington, D. C. to carry out his wishes. His mortal remains were cremated as requested and essence of his Earthly form was placed in an Urn and interned in Arlington National Cemetary, Arlington, Virginia. He would have preferred to have his ashes scattered but this is no longer permitted by law. There was no funeral, just a simple graveside service with Chaplain Captain David F. Tate, from Fort Myer officiating.

This prayer, which had been handed to the Chaplain, was read with deep feeling at the conclusion of the service.

We gather here in humble gratitude to the Creator of all forms for the privilege of knowing and working with so great a servant of the Divine Father.

As the essence of the mortal form returns to the Earth from whence it came we reverently dedicate our lives to the Cause for which George Adamski so nobly lived.

We ask our Heavenly Father for the wisdom and the Courage to continue to bring to mankind the understanding and the beauty granted to each individual and so simply taught by His obedient servant.

Our lives are richer for knowing George Adamski the man for he shared his understanding of Cosmic Intelligence with all who would listen. And now, as he lives in a greater field of service, may we as mortals be ever mindful of the Symbol for Life for which he so unselfishly lived and died.

His name is a symbol of hope, of understanding in the midst of confusion, a promise of happiness and Life Eternal when Nature's Cosmic Laws are obeyed. Amen.

I wonder how many realize that he was a member of the Interplanetary Council. This is a group of men of high Cosmic Conscious Awareness that evaluate the conditions of our system and keeps their representatives informed of the changes. The Brothers who travel in ships and those here on this planet are liaison men that carry this information.

Due to George Adamski's unwavering loyalty in carrying out his every commission, The Council decided to grant him a new body through which to work. As the mortal form of George Adamski was of the Earth it had to be returned to the Earth, but there has not been a break in his intelligence as he carries on his work in a new form.

I have been asked if George Adamski is re-born as a baby and my answer was no. When an individualised intelligence is as aware of Cosmic Consciousness as his was, this is not necessary. There is nothing fantastic about this when the Laws Of The Cosmos are understood.

Do not be saddened by his passing for he is very much among us and the Brothers are still at the helm guiding and directing our lives. So rejoice and give thanks to the Creator for granting him a new body through which he can work unhampered.

---Alice K. Wells

A TRIBUTE TO GEORGE ADAMSKI
by
Desmond Leslie
(Co-Author: "FLYING SAUCERS HAVE LANDED")

Of all the people in the flying saucer world, George Adamski stands alone as its most controversial character. Many others have claimed contacts and been treated with tolerance, belief or amused contempt, but George had only to open his mouth to bring down a storm of abuse, praise and wonderment.

Perhaps I came to know him as well as anybody, I stayed with him several times and discovered facets in his character seldom revealed in public. Underneath the talkative, colorful exterior lurked a very great human being. Some quirk in his nature often took pains to conceal this and present instead, as his public face, a far more shallow person than he really was.

Who was he?

Certainly no ordinary person. Physically he was Polish with, I think a touch of Romany. Immensely strong, good looking and with burning black eyes. Spiritually he was more than one person. There was George of the public lectures--the one I liked least for he tried to say too much all at once. Then there was the relaxed, naughty George with a keen eye for a pretty face, and a pluckish delight in shocking the profaced and prudes.

Then there was another George, beautifully spoken, wise, kind, and deeply aware of the importance of his task. Through this George, I several times glimpsed the presence of a Master, and I was always sorry when the curtain came down again and the worldly mask obscured him.

I often wondered why he should have been singled out as the prime prophet of saucery. He believed that he had reincarnated from another planet through karmic reasons to give his teachings, and I find that idea quite acceptable. He believed that others, greater in the world's esteem, had also been contacted and given the same mission, but that for various personal reasons had refused or failed. He saw himself as the 'lame the halt and the blind' who were called to the King's feast after the chosen guests had made excuses not to come. He felt that he was a broken reed, but alas the only reed willing to try and play their tune. So with all his might, with his inability to write and speak good English, and the inate difficulties of being the character that he was, he set out undaunted by criticism or abuse to give the message as best he saw it.

GO IN PEACE!

This seems to me most probable, even a wise move on the part of the Brothers. To choose a great and respected person would be too easy for us to accept, or too difficult for that person who might be demoted and declared mad. Again, in George Adamski were all the virtues and failings of this planet, slightly over-life-sized. So that one could recognize an aspect of oneself in him and judge from a more personal basis.

To assess the validity of his claims is still difficult, I am personally completely satisfied that his photos and early contacts are completely authentic and will in time be proven by later events. Some of his claims take a lot of swallowing. But just when you had decided to write him off as a babbler, something turns up to substantiate them. For instance when I first visited him in 1954, he spoke of the Van Allen Belts, and the 'Fireflies in space' as later seen by the cosmonaunts. Neither of these were known at the time. The last time I saw him he calmly announced: 'I saw Pope John yesterday.' Well, as it happened I was able to get independent confirmation that this was true. John gave him a beautiful gold medallion effigy of himself which as far as I know has never yet been released and is only given to the most special people. George claimed to have given John a sealed package from the Brothers with advice for the conduct of the Council. Certainly the way the Church has behaved since then is very much in line with the Brothers' policies.

That was the maddening thing about George. Just as you thought you had at last caught him in a whopper, something would turn up to substaintiate his claim.

I remember two occasions on successive nights at Palomar when I saw a tiny golden remote control disk leave rapidly. On the second occasion we were talking on his patio just after dark when I got a tremendous feeling of being watched. I turned around just in time to see a tiny golden disk not more than fifty feet away, as it shot upward in a trail of light.

George laughed, and I said: "Thank God our converstation has been clean the last twenty minutes."

He refused to ask me on a 'contact' with him and at the time it peeved me greatly. But I realized later that I was in no fit spiritual state for such an experience and had I been taken aboard a saucer I doubt if I'd have been a very successful prophet afterwards for my ego is highly susceptible to spiritual aggrandizement. Many who have genuine contacts have gone very odd, forming new religions and in fact doing everything the Brothers desire least. I doubt I would have been any exception.

One thing I liked about George was his utter down-to-earthiness. I don't think he ever suffered from spiritual pride -- from abuse, from strain, from many other things, yes -- but despite the warring human factions which grew up among his followers, there was always a great modesty and sense of his own unimportance in scheme of such vastness and splendor.

I don't suppose he will mind me telling this, now that he has cast off the fine old body, but he once showed me the most extraordinary birthmark. His navel was not like a human navel at all. It was a huge solar disk with deeply cut rays extending out about six inches all around it, from waist to groin. What this signifies I have no idea - unless it is truly a sign of a 'Child of the Sun'

Anyone who knew him grew to love him immensely. Our first contact was so strange. I had 'Flying Saucers Have Landed' being rejected by publisher after publisher, when I heard through a friend of the first desert contact a week previously. I immediately wrote to George asking if he would let me see and possibly buy his photographs for my book. He replied by sending me the whole remarkable set of pictures, along with permission to use them without fee. I thought what an extraordinary man. He takes the most priceless pictures of all time and wants no money for them. Later he sent me his manuscript humbly suggesting I might be able to find a publisher for it. By this time dear Waveney Girvin had accepted my book and was perturbed that if we used George's pictures and synopsis of his story with our own, George's book wouldn't stand a chance; and after much soul searching suggested a joint publication. We wrote off to George who cabled back the following day before receiving our letter, "Agree to a joint publication." Here indeed was telepathy at work! And so the amazing relationship developed. When we met again physcally we were old friends, as if in some former life we had been very close. His devoted friend and housekeeper Alice Wells was also an amazing lady. You never had to tell her or ask anything. She knew. She'd pick up your thought and answer it in advance.

George claimed that many thousands of more mature souls who'd once lived on the Earth where returning both in flying saucers and by rebirth to help our planet through its time of trial. It seems very likely that George was one of them, and that he was chosen to confound the intellectual and the arrogant and the know-alls just as the prophets in the past have been chosen whose very simplicity and humble birth has made them better vehicles for a spiritual message than those who reasoning powers have clogged up their spiritual channels.

We shall miss George. Miss him very much, but I cannot feel sad at his going. He gave his utmost to the work and the world will never be quite the same place again, richer for his coming, a little poorer for his going. But I don't believe by any means that we have seen the last of him. If he is reborn on another planet he has promised to come back and contact us when possible.

With George anything could happen. And usually does!

Dear Old Space Man--Go in Peace!

"When a thing is hidden away with so much pains, merely to reveal it is to destroy it."
　-----Tertullian

The Greatest Saucer Story Ever Told

Gray Barker

The monks had just finished roasting a sheep and the Abbott was ready to say grace when one of the brethern of the monastary came running in, shouting about a great portent in the heavens.

The Abbott forced his portly form into a trot, ran into the courtyard, and there was the flying saucer:

"Lo! a large round silvery thing like a disk flew slowly over them and excited the greatest terror."

One beauty of this very ancient account is its classical unfological consistency. Somebody sees a saucer and goes to the prevailing Authorities for an explanation. In this case, of course the ruling intellectual authority of the very small monastic community was the Abbott.

Faced with the question, the Abbott came up with an explanation which puts the colorless Air Force Explainers to shame:

"Whereat Henry the Abbott immediately cried that Wilfred was an adulterer, wherefore it was impious to....."

Wilfred, whoever he was, had been the fellow who supplied the sheep, and whether he really had been guilty of such activities, we shall never know -- but the Abbott's pre-Kinsey observation immortalized (or IMMORALIZED) him forever, or at least practically forever.

For this happened in A. D. 1290.

Although not the greatest saucer story ever told, surely it was one of the earliest, and this old account appears in the beginning of a book which caused world-wide awareness of flying saucer visitations.

In 1952, Desmond Leslie, cousin of Winston Churchill, and a playwright, had been trying to get a publisher for a book he had written -- after doing years of research among rare manuscripts. Leslie said it proved that flying saucers, which Kenneth Arnold had publicized in 1947, were nothing new, and had been around since the dawn of recorded history.

Several publishers read the manuscript and turned it down flat. Some said it was "too crakpot," others "too scientific," and the rest said nobody would be interested in reading it.

In November of 1952, however, Leslie's fortunes changed -- by a dramatic happening which transpired thousands of miles away from his London home. On the 20th of that month George Adamski met a man from outer space on a California desert!

Publishers in New York and London sat up and took notice, and promptly purchased Adamski's account of his space visitation. The manuscript was too short for a book-length publication, however, and quite by accident T. Werner Laurie, Ltd., of London, remembered the Leslie manuscript which had been kicking around.

By combining the two manuscripts the British publisher came up with FLYING SAUCERS HAVE LANDED.

At latest count, the U. S. edition has gone through twelve printings and had sold over half a million copies!

In the meantime the George Adamski story had been translated into many languages and had caused controversy all over the world.

VIMANAS AND VENUSIANS

A review of what happened to George Adamski is best told by actually reviewing this strange book itself.

Desmond Leslie begins the book with the old account of the monastary sighting; then he relates a succession of similar accounts beginning in 1619, and extending through the centuries to publication deadline.

Then Leslie delves even farther back into antiquity!

Ancient manuscripts, dating back through prehistory to Atlantean days, not only tell of man-made flying saucers very much like those now in the skies, but GIVE RATHER COMPLETE DIRECTIONS FOR BUILDING THEM!

The Vimanas (air-boats) of the Atlanteans were constructed of either wood or metal, were propelled by engines utilizing mercury, though the exact methods of propulsion are not given. The energy was directed through nozzles or jets, turned in different directions to steer the craft. Although the vimanas could travel at only 100 miles per hour, it is hinted advanced machines could travel to the planets. Apparently Noah's Flood, a catastrophe running through the histories and traditions of peoples throughout the world, wiped out these ancient saucer-building civilizations as well as their wonderous flying machines.

Mention of weapons of war similar to modern atomics can also be found in ancient manuscripts, Leslie declares. He feels the asteroid belt may once have been a planet whose scientists succeeded in blowing themselves skyward.

Nor were all the saucers of old propelled by what we might today consider physical means. Pointing to Saint Teresa of Avila, reported to be able to rise in the air, the author believes she may have mastered an amazing and abundant kind of power, the control of sound, whereby uttering or producing certain kinds of wave lengths could oppose gravity and cause a body or building stone to be levitated. If a properly pitched note can break a mirror, "is it beyond the realms of possibility that if sound were completely understood....it might be harmonized to the electrical magnetic forces that produce levitations?" Leslie suggested that prehistoric flying saucers were literally "flown with a song," and the modern counterpart man
modern counterpart may utilize similar secrets of tapping the energies of the universe. The mystical "Abracadabras" and "Open Sesames" of legendary magicians may be half-remembered sounds which could move mountains and build the Great Pyramid.

That might explain how the fifteen-ton polished casing stones of the Great Pyramid were lifted and fitted to incredible tolerances without modern machinery, that is, IF it would be possible, even _with_ modern machinery.

If great natural sources of

THE GREATEST SAUCER STORY EVER TOLD

power in the universe could be tapped by the ancient, why could not the same be done today? Although Leslie shares the views of many occultists that the realms of what many term the supernatural may one day be the great frontier of science, it is difficult for scientists to discard preconceived methods which lead them against a stone wall. As an example, the author points to electricity and asks what it <u>really</u> is, remarking that so far scientists have been unable to tell him what makes his TV set <u>actually</u> work, though they are experts at building circuits to control the electricity flowing through its tubes. Although engineers can tell him much about the <u>how</u>, Leslie thinks an understanding of the <u>why</u> would lead to far greater

But man's understanding of his enviroment and limitless possibilities are expanding, At one time it was believed the human body would disintergrate if the horse were abandoned for the fantastic speed of locomotives; later the sonic barrier, through which no plane could pass without supposed disintegration, was penetrated; now the speed of light is deemed unsurpassable.

So with the scientific fancy freed from mundane limiting horizons, the reader is thus prepared for and ushered into the second part of the book, wherein one George Adamski actually meets a space visitor and draws an amazing discourse from him.

Adamski lived at Palomar Gardens, 3,000 feet in altitude, on the slopes of Mt. Palomar, where the 200-inch telescope is located. Describing himself as "philosopher, student, teacher, and saucer researcher," he took care to point out that he had no connection with the staff of the observatory. Although his regular occupation was not stated, Adamski was connected with the restaurant at Palomar Gardens, though not the owner of it. He also said he had no college degrees.

Adamski first became interested in space craft in October, 1946, when during a meteor shower he saw an object like a giant dirigible in the sky, which soon pointed upward and shot out of view with a burst of flame. At the time he thought little of it, but the widespread talk of flying saucers, after Kenneth Arnold saw them in 1947, led him to watch the skies. With two telescopes, one of which had a camera attached, Adamski said he was able to observe and photograph hundreds of saucers, though few of the photographs turned out well. Remarking about the comment of some people who wonder why he saw so many saucers, he said that anyone can see them if he forms the habit of watching the sky. "These ships are there and they can be seen by those who look up whenever they are out of doors -- not always, but sooner or later the searcher will be rewarded."

THE MAN FROM OUTER SPACE

But it was on November 20, 1952, at 12:30 noon, that Adamski got his closest look at a saucer, and talked with a long-haired man from Venus. Hearing that saucers had been landing in nearby deserts, presumably from groups of persons who had allegedly contacted the occupants, Adamski decided to try his own luck. Gathering four friends, his secretary and the proprietor of the restaurant, he set forth early one morning. The party consisted of Mr. and Mrs. A. C. Bailey, of Winslow, Arizona; Mrs. Alice K. Wells, owner of Plamar Gardens and operator of the restaurant; Dr. and Mrs. George H. Williamson, of Prescott, Arizona, and Mrs. Lucy McGinnis, his secretary. Adamski located the meeting spot, on a desert about ten miles from Desert Center toward Parker, Arizona, mainly by hunch, since he had developed the habit of following hunches or feelings. Stopping for a picnic lunch, the party noticed considerable aircraft circling the vicinity and then a large cigar-shaped craft. Following another hunch, Adamski told the rest of

The Venusian, as observed by Alice K. Wells, who witnessed desert contact through binoculars. Her rough sketch of spacemen has been redrawn above by Gene Duplantier.

the party to wait while he went to a spot about a half mile from the highway. The ship seemed to follow the car as they drove him part of the distance to the location, then stopped when the car stopped.

Adamski spotted a small saucer drifting through a saddle be-tween two mountain peaks and hurriedly turned his telescope on it, shooting pictures. Then the saucer disappeared. But soon afterward he was aware of a figure beckoning to him, which, upon closer observation, proved to be the person from the space ship.

The man had long hair, finely chiseled features, and was dressed in an odd one-piece suit, apparently without seams. The trousers resembled ski pants, were rather full and were held at the ankles as if by close-fitting bands. So were the arms drawn in at the wrists, and a band fitted around the waist. The man appeared to be about 28 years old and to weigh one hundred thirty five pounds, was about five feet, six inches tall.

The man appeared friendly, was smiling, and Adamski hurriedly tried communicating with him. Although the person spoke in an odd language somewhat like Chinese and didn't understand English, Adamski stated he was able to talk to him through sign language and mental telepathy.

He had come there from Venus, it developed, though flying saucers came from many different planets, including those in our own solar system and from outside. All of the planets in our solar system are inhabited, according to the visitor, and his job appeared to be checking on radia-tions caused by atomic bombs. To express the danger of the bombs to our own earth, the visitor pointed to the ground and said, "Boom! Boom!" The man believed in God, though led Adamski to believe that on his planet people adhere more to the laws of the Creator than man does on materialistic earth. Physically, men from all over the universe are much alike, the visitor observed.

STRANGE FOOTPRINTS

The Vensian objected to being photographed, so Adamski didn't insist; though the man asked for one of the photographic plates that had been exposed earlier,

THE GREATEST SAUCER STORY EVER TOLD

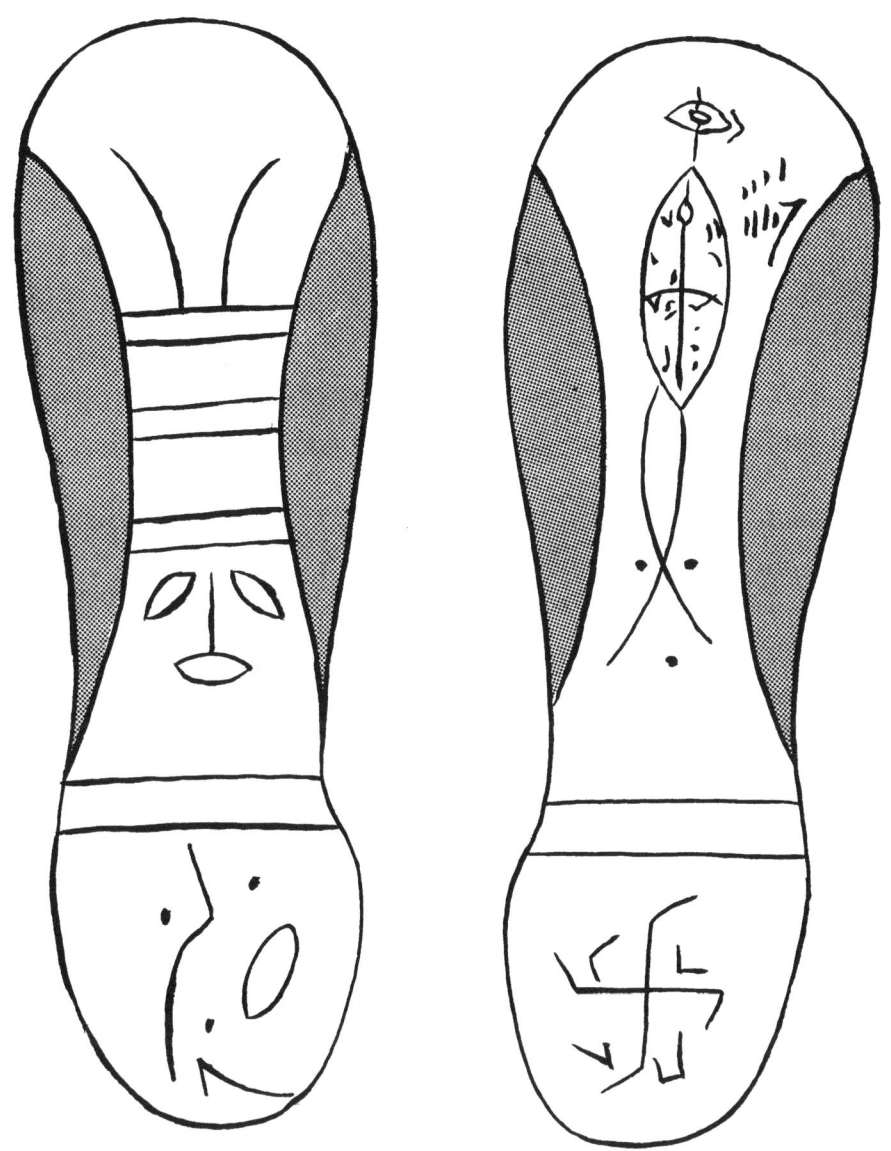

Above: Strange footprints left on desert by Venusian, redrawn by Gene Duplantier from original sketch by witness Alice K. Wells. Although there have been many interpretations of the symbols, their exact meaning has never been established.

promising to return it later. Refusing the disappointed Adamski a ride in the saucer, which was nearby, the visitor concluded the interview, got into the contraption and sailed away. Twenty-three days later the saucer buzzed Palomar Gardens and dropped the photographic plate to the ground. Upon development it disclosed curious writing, reproduced in the book.

The visitor also left footprints at the site of the desert meeting (see illustration) and casts of these were made with plaster of Paris, disclosing more symbolic markings. Experts the world over tried to decipher the messages and many different "translations" appeared in print.

Although the desert photographs were spoiled, apparently by radiation from the craft, the pictures taken of the saucer on its return visit are corkers. They show the saucer in great detail, including interesting ball-type landing gear, and also are reproduced in the book.

I have tried to sum up the book in a literal manner because there is little chance of proving or disproving either part of it. Leslie's theories of early saucers are connected with ancient manuscripts, admitting of a pay-your-money-and-take-your-choice interpretation. We hereby refuse to get into the subject of ancient manuscripts, for the present saucer situation is confusing enough; and our profound ignorance of the various ologies involved is enough to make us throw up our hands. Even if they could be discredited, Leslie's theories are so darned interesting we don't want to try and kick them around.

As far as picking Adamski's story apart, we believe that also is quite impossible.

Apparently Adamski had witnesses, but they were a half mile away. One of them had a movie camera, and Adamski does have a good excuse for not photographing the cigar-shaped craft. While it was hovering the lady with the camera was too nervous to adjust the camera; by the time she did adjusted it, the ship was moving.

Adamski doesn't mention whether they shot any movies of the meeting, but maybe it was too far away. One of the witnesses did watch the proceedings through binoculars and was able to draw a sketch of the visitor. (see illustration.)

As I read the exciting story for the first time, I did get the impression of a tone of great honesty throughout Adamski's account, and could hardly doubt that he was telling the truth as he knew it.

The story, however, was almost too fantastic to believe. I tried to come up with an explanation which would satisfy myself. Maybe there was a flying saucer, and an alien life form, but perhaps the interpretation of such stimuli could have been much different if seen from the viewpoint of a different observer. The religious tone of the experience was evidenced by Adamski's remark, "Yet there was and is an inexpressable joy for the privilege. I had been given a glimpse of friends from a world beyond this earth -- and the ecstasy of a visit with one of them." Evidently it was an experience of worshipful adoration, much the same as may have happened, we felt, many times in the past, to people who wrote religious works.

After all, there had been no communication by actual language as we know it; talking had been done with sign language and telepathy, both admitting of possible errors of interpretation. And more and more we believed that saucers came nearest being that which is "all things to all men."

We wonder if saucerians behave much like terrestrials _believe_ they _should_ behave.

The little men seen by devilish terrestrials probably have horns.

So it was greatly to Adamski's credit, by this line of reasoning, that the visitors appeared to be kind and good, Christ-like in demeanor and speech.

FACT OR FICTION?

If our inferences were logical, surely Adamski, regardless of what he saw that day in the desert, and how accurately he reported the occurrence, had a charitable and benign soul. For he saw only good coming to mankind from the saucers, a reflection, perhaps, of his own hopes and ideals.

Thus were my feelings when I first read what I still consider to be "the greatest saucer story ever told."

Fact? Fiction? Many flying saucer researchers will give you a quick answer, claiming one of the two alternatives, To me it was never quite so simple.

If George Adamski told the truth we personally think it was of the experiences written in FLYING SAUCERS HAVE LANDED. We believe his photographs, published in that book, are also real.

Encouraged by public demand for more facts, and excited by the publicity obtained from the best-seller, did Adamski manufacture further incidents we wrote about in his second

ARLINGTON NATIONAL CEMETERY

This cemetery is situated on the south side of the Potomac River in the State of Virginia, just opposite the City of Washington, D.C. The cemetery was established in 1864 and is administered by the Department of the Army, Office of the Chief of Support Services and under the immediate supervision of the Commanding General, Military District of Washington.

May 1984

Map of Arlington National Cemetery, as supplied by the Department of the Army, showing exact location of Adamski's Grave.

NAME _George Adamski_
GRAVE _295_
SECTION _43_

Approximate location of grave is indicated in red.

Entrance gates will be open and visitors permitted in the Cemetery every day throughout the year during the following hours:

October thru March   8:00 A.M. to 5:00 P.M.
April thru September   8:00 A.M. to 7:00 P.M.

GENERAL INFORMATION

1. Cemetery *will not* be used as picnic grounds.
2. Visitors *will not* litter the grounds, cut, break or injure trees, shrubs or plants or otherwise conduct themselves in a manner not in keeping with the dignity and the sacredness of the Cemetery.
3. All graves will be decorated during the 24-hour period preceding Memorial Day with small flags, which will be removed immediately after Memorial Day.
4. Flags *are not* permitted on graves at any other time.
5. Cut flowers, wreaths or floral emblems either live or artificial, with or without wire stand, may be placed on graves at any time, provided that the wire stand is more than two feet from the headstone, and that cut flowers, wreaths or floral emblems *do not* touch headstone.
6. Information regarding removal of floral items will be furnished by Superintendent.

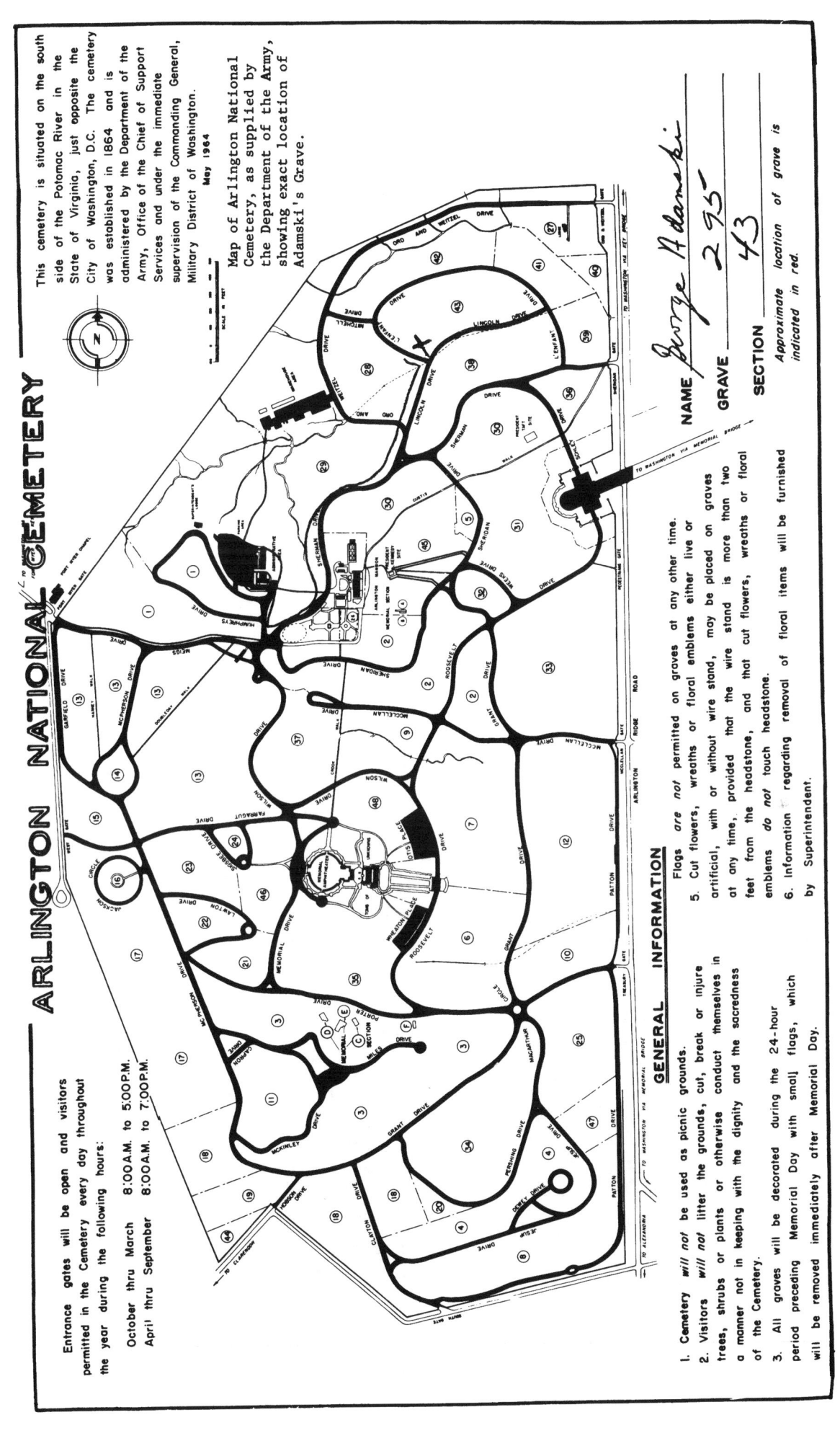

book, INSIDE THE SPACE SHIPS?

In the latter Adamski claimed to take rides in space ships, and his narrative became more contrived. His photographs in the second book were highly questionable.

We have our own pet theory which applies equally to people who contact space people, to mediums, and even to poltergeists. Something real, though weird and fantastic, happens to an individual and he tells the world about it. People come from miles to hear the story, and then want to hear more. A medium has a few tremendous materialization seances, but can't turn them "on" at will. A poltergeist starts throwing things around a house, people hear about it and come to see.

The saucer "contactee" may simply concoct further accounts, not wishing to disappoint his public. The medium, who can't always effect materialization, buys some cheesecloth. The adolescent in the house where the mischeivious spirit is hurling vases gets the idea that he or she should perpetuate the phenomena that that he or she subconsciously caused in the first place. So the child throws some things around and is caught at it. "Fake!" the public cries.

George Adamski is expelled from his membership in the National Investigations Committee On Aerial Phenomena. The organization, headed by Major Donald E. Keyhoe, is apparently frightened of the import of his story and uses as an excuse his later accounts which do not have the ring of truth that the original had.

Many cease to believe in George Adamski. They call him a crackpot, as they rush to some new medium, or to see some new poltergeist.

And maybe the Space People, if indeed they be real, are smiling with satisfaction. Perhaps they wanted to cause public awareness of flying saucers, but not TOO MUCH of an awareness. Perhaps they wanted to prepare the public GENTLY for what is to occur.

While many "objective" and "scientific" saucer researchers screamed that Adamski was perpetrating a hoax, there was not one among them when, pinned down, could say anything personally bad about him.

For George charmed his critics wherever he roamed. No matter how vitrolic his adversaries, he maintained a pleasant attitude which challenged their negativity. Maybe this was one reason why they could never cope with him!

I had corresponded with Adamski on many occasions and felt I knew him fairly well, and always looked forward to the personal meeting I felt was inevitable. But I waited too long. On the evening of April 23, 1965, George died, of a heart attack, in Silver Springs, Maryland.

****

On July 15, one of the hottest days of the scorching summer of 1966, I drove to Arlington National Cemetary with the wife of the owner of a business I work for. I had taken her there to see the Lee Mansion and the Kennedy grave.

While there I remembered that Adamski was said to be buried there, and I went to the Cemetery office to inquire. I was given a map, with the number and location of his grave clearly marked.

The owner's wife and the boss, who also was along on the trip, never did quite understand who George Adamski was, or why I was searching for the grave -- though I tried to explain. I think they still believe it to be that of some relative of mine.

Once I found the grave, I stood there looking at the inscription.

A cloud came over the hot sun, bringing a moment of coolness. I felt suddenly relaxed, from the tension of the long day of museum-going and sightseeing. I asked the owner's wife to take a picture of me, standing beside the headstone.

THE GREATEST SAUCER STORY EVER TOLD

Just then another car pulled up behind our own on the nearby driveway, and a young couple got out. Smiling, they walked toward us. They were "looking for George" too.

They had come from Canada, just to visit the grave, and it made me somewhat ashamed to mentally note that I had made the visit mainly as an afterthought.

"We have enjoyed his books so much," the woman told me, "and we wanted so much to see where he laid."

They had picked some wildflowers from a friend's estate in nearby Alexandria, and she had made this into a wreath, which she layed on the grave.

A wind came up and blew at the delicate flowers.

I knew that soon they would die and wither away, as had some others that some unknown person had placed on the grave, apparently days before.

But George Adamski's story, whether fact or fiction, would never die.

It would excite others, as it had me, and inspire them too. They might end up disbelieving what he had said, but meanwhile they would have delved deeply into the mysteries of the universe and our role on this planet.

Whether or not they had really believed in George Adamski, their research had purged them of many devils. It had thrown light into darkened corners where the Three Men in Black lurk, and cringe in terror at a shaft of sunlight.

Gray Barker, at the grave of George Adamski, in Arlington National Cemetery.

The cursed darkness of fear, repression and superstition had been pushed back somewhat, as they laughed and enjoyed the fellowship of other friends who had also studied in the same avenues.

They didn't entirely believe in the Space Men as such any longer, because they finally realized that THEY, THEMSELVES, were space men and women.

And they would return intermittenly to the grave of George Adamski, not quite knowing why, not quite knowing that, allegorically, a great man had given them great truths.

They would not realize that almost two thousand years ago another man had handled the truth the very same way.

"Science of today -- the superstition of tomorrow. Science of tomorrow -- the superstition of today."
-----Charles Fort

Photographic Expert:

"Adamski's Photos Are Real"

Michael G. Mann

"Oh him, he was a phoney. You could tell from the way he talked."

" I knew he was making it up all along."

These and like statements have spread far and wide since the death of George Adamski. Ray D'Aquila of UFO Contact Group in the Netherlands who originally supported George now states, ... "I do not support Mr. Adamski's statements full 100% any more. There is no saying where truth ends and fiction begins....."

Many of Adamski's followers have deserted his teachings.

Those of you who know me realize that my main interest in Ufology is saucer photographs. Without question Adamski had compiled the greatest and most interesting collection of UFO photos in the field. He claimed to have taken these pictures personally during his meetings with the space beings who piloted these crafts.

While I am not qualified to judge, nor am I interested in judging Adamski's contact accounts and books, I AM in a position to analyze his photos scientifically.

Many look at the photographs and consider them excellent renditions of tin cans, models and toys. "Yankee" magazine went so far as to construct a ball shaped model from a coffee can, hub cap and three ping pong balls. They photographed it and concocted a contact story to go with the photo. The fact that people believed their phony report proved in THEIR minds that Adamski's tale was likewise, untrue. If this line of reasoning were logical it would mean that if I were to construct a model of a TWA 707 Fanjet and photograph the model, all such jets would cease to exist. I am sure that TWA isn't worrying about the situation!

Let's examine the facts of the Adamski phenomena. Adamski took a series of photos of bell and cigar

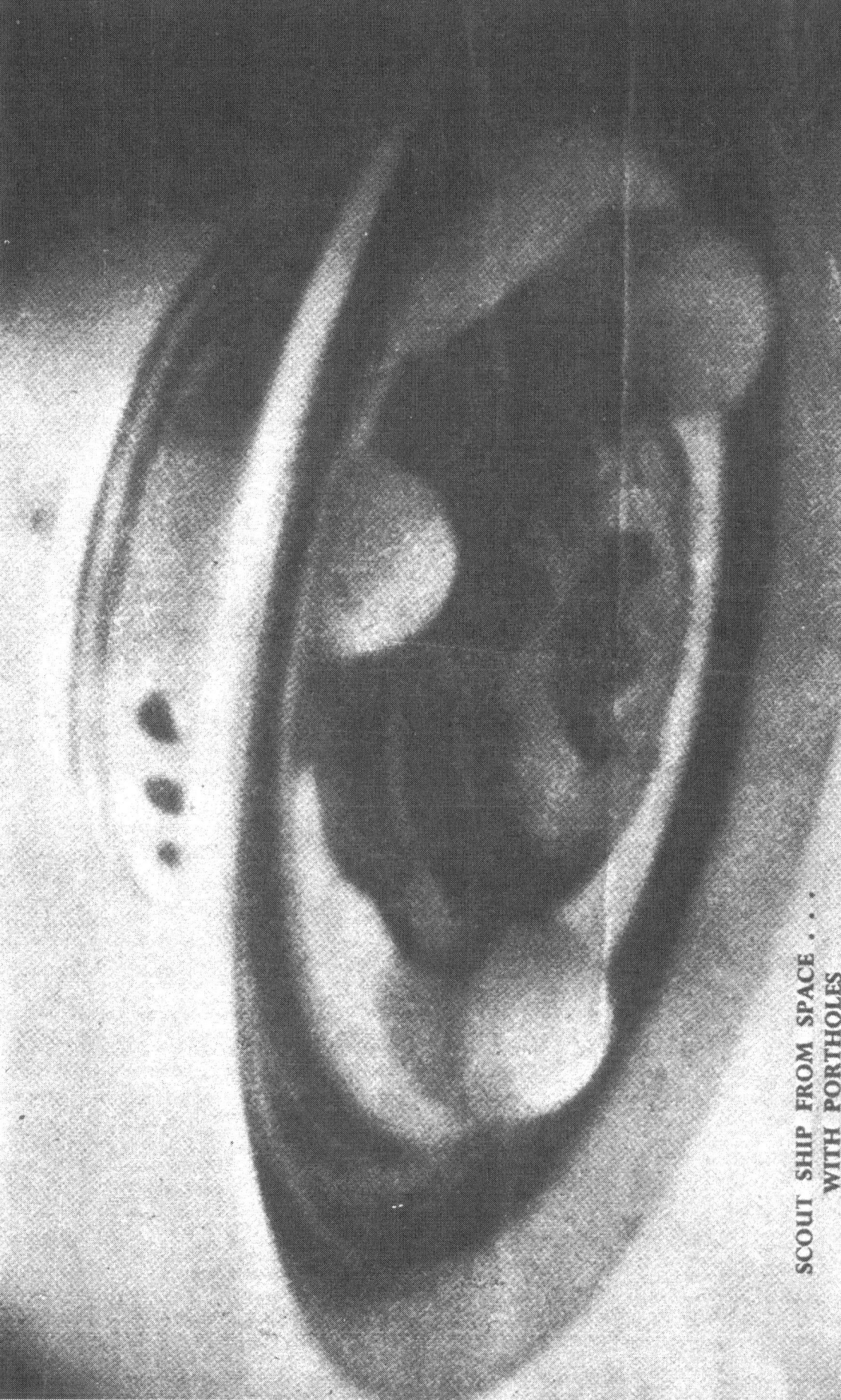

SCOUT SHIP FROM SPACE . . . . WITH PORTHOLES

George Adamski says he took this picture at Palomar Gardens, California, through his six-inch telescope at 9.10 a.m. on December 13 last year. It is claimed to be a Venusian flying saucer, about thirty-five feet in diameter, and made of translucent metal. There are portholes and three "landing spheres"

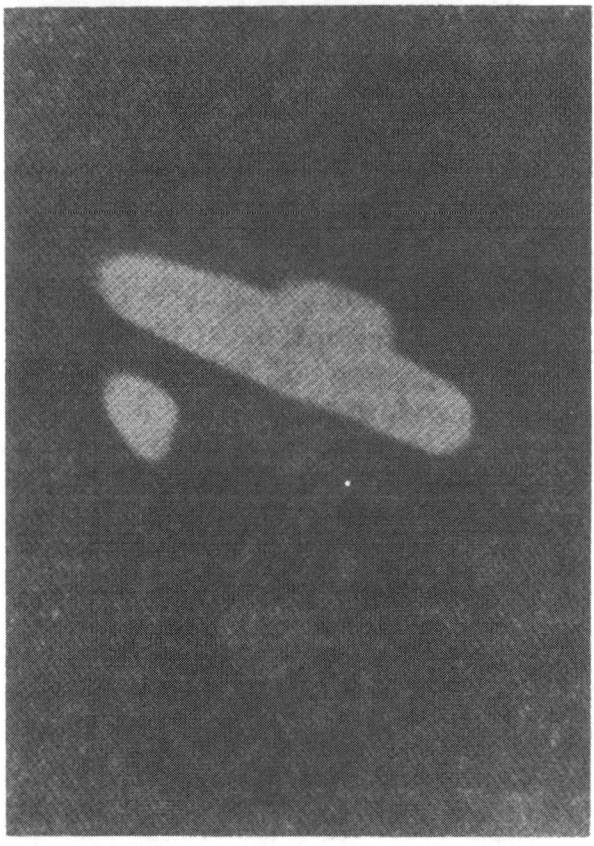

Top: One of the Adamski photos of bell-shaped craft. Bottom: Bell-shaped object photographed by astronaut Scott Carpenter from space capsule (Courtesy Michael G. Mann)

shaped craft. Very similar objects have been photographed by Cedric Allingham, Howard Menger, George Stock, Dr. Daniel W. Fry, Robert Coe Gardner, George Van Tassel, Paul Trent, and scores of other people. It is quite evident that Adamski was not the only person to see the photograph this shape of craft.

There are three cases in particular that I would like to recount, which tend to verify the Adamski case.

The first has to do with a rather blurry photograph taken by Sgt. Jerrold E. Baker. The picture shows what seems to be the bottom of a saucer which looks amazingly similar to the Adamski type craft. The blurry aspect is understandable and in fact helps to substantiate the sighting due to the fact that the object was moving rapidly and photographed with a brownie box camera. Brownies have a lens speed of 1/25th of a second, and therefore a speedy object would appear as a blur in an exposure. The interesting thing is that this photo was taken on December 13, 1952, at about nine thirteen AM. This was about three minutes after George had taken his famous bell craft photo a short distance away at Palomar Gardens.

The second bit of photo corroboration is the picture taken by astronaut Scott Carpenter. This strange object was sighted by the astronauts near their Gemini space capsule and looks amazingly bell shaped.

The third photo I will deal with was taken by thirteen year old Stephen Darbshire, son of a Dr. Darbshire of Coninston, England.

It was on the morning of February 15, 1954, that young Stephen, of Coniston, Lancashire, seemed to have an uncontrollable urge to climb a hill behind his home. He and his

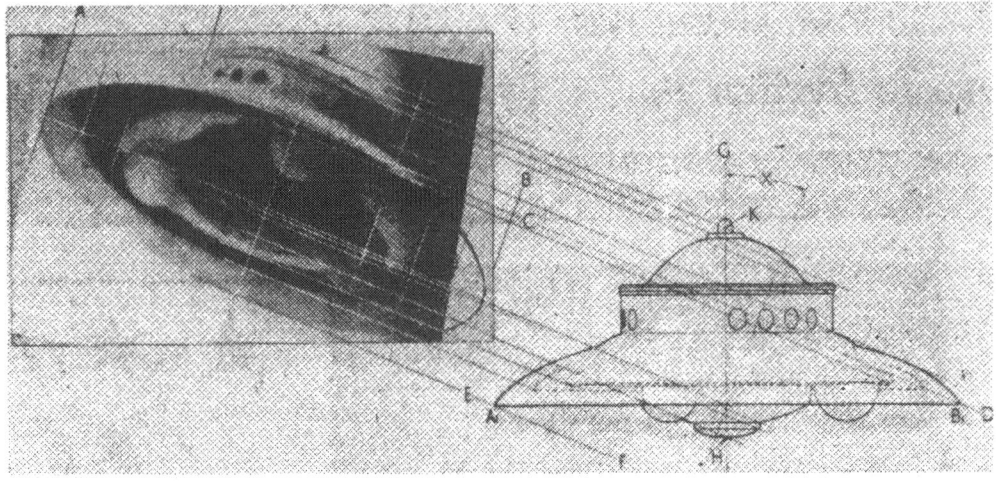

Comparison of the Adamski (top) Coniston (lower) photographs

A description by Leonard Cramp of his drawing method.

A-B represents the unforeshortened diameters.

C-E represents the foreshortened diameters.

If we make two marks, distance A-B apart, on the edge of a piece of paper and turn the paper so that the marks lie one on each of the two lines C-D and E-F, at A1 and B1, this will represent the disc at the photographed angle. But viewed from one side it will be shown as a straight line.

By bisecting this and drawing a right angle G-H, we now have the vertical axis of the ship, on to which the true height H-K can be projected. The angle X can be measured off and that will be the angle which the ship made with the camera when photographed.

From this it will be seen that the rest is simply repetition of the above.

When the various points are connected up as in the diagrams, we have then a fairly accurate orthographic view.

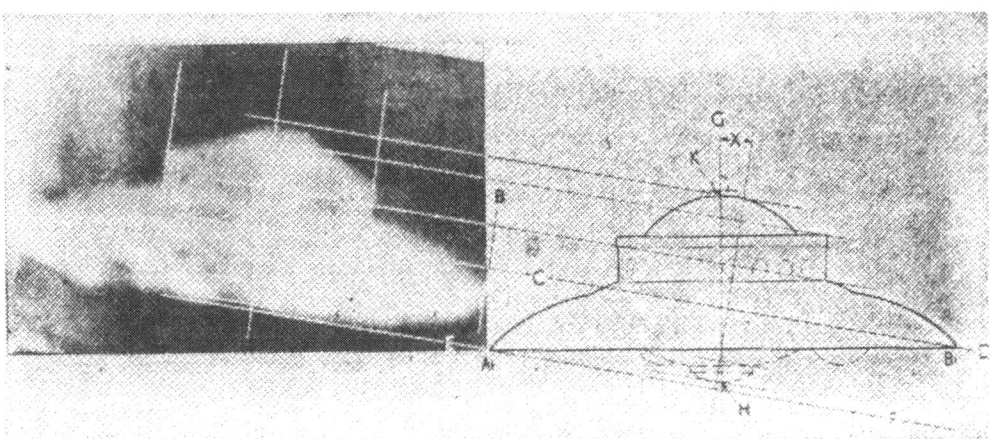

eight-year-old cousin, Adrian Myer, went up the hill, taking a small camera along in the hope of taking bird pictures, since bird watching was his principal hobby.

Suddenly Adrian shouted, "Look at that thing!" And there it was, coming from a direction of the sun a strange silvery round object. It descended to earth about a hundred yards away and disappeared behind some rising ground, came into view again a few seconds later. Then it suddenly tipped up on its side and shot up into the sky with a swishing sound, the only noise it made during its appearance.

In his excitement, investigation showed Stephen had set his camera on "bulb" instead of the intended 1/25 second, and had taken about a one-second exposure. As a result, the picture was blurred.

"It was a solid metal-like thing with a dome, portholes, and three bumps or landing domes underneath. In the center the underneath was darker and pointed like a cone. At first three portholes were visible but then it turned slightly and we saw four. There was what looked like a hatch on top of the cabin dome."

Stephen also described the objects as 40 feet in diameter and presenting a silvery, glassy appearance, "like metal or plastic which light goes through but which you can't see through" (He likely meant translucent). He also said that it had a ball-type landing gear.

At first Stephen's father, a doctor, did not believe him, but was convinced after the photograph was developed. Young Stephen was interviewed by newspaper men and saucer investigators, but stuck to his orig-

"ADAMSKI'S PHOTOS ARE REAL"

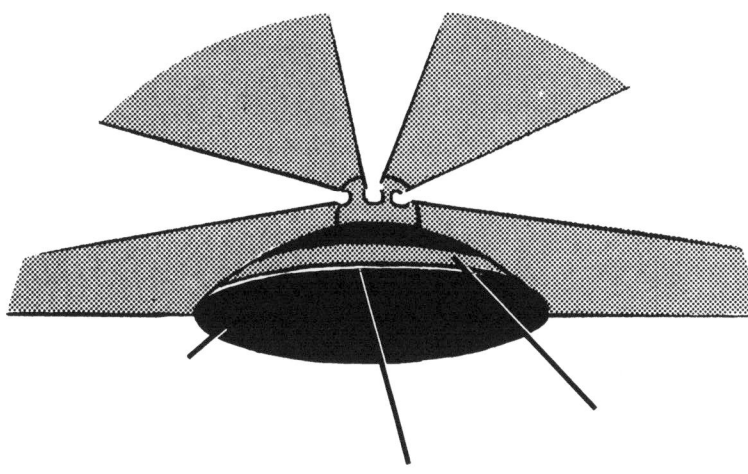

Right: Sketch made by F. W. Potter of "Adamski type" saucer and redrawn by Gene Duplantier. Worldside sightings of similar craft tend to confirm Adamski's photographs.

inal story.

Although his description of the saucer fitted that allegedly photographed by Adamski, Stephen's parents confirmed his statement that he never read the Leslie--Adamski book, FLYING SAUCERS HAVE LANDED, nor had he seen even an abridged account. He did say, however, he had seen Adamski's photograph in the London Illustrated, Stephen said the saucer had four port holes, but the photograph he had seen, which had been trimmed down for reproduction, showed only three (the fourth had been cut off).

An orthographic projection of this photo shows that the object has the exact proportions of the Adamski craft. Coincidence is so fantastic in this case it is just out of the question.

Pev Marley, ace cameraman for Cecil B. DeMille, and photo expert pointed out "Adamski's pictures if faked are the cleverest ever seen, rivaling a Houdini"..... "The shadows on these saucers and also on the ground correspond to such a degree that they could not be faked."

A recent issue of "FLYING SAUCER REVIEW" of England has come to the defense of the memory of George Adamski, In their report they listed many of the cases that corroborated Adamski's stories. In particular they mentioned a Mr. F. W. Potter as having sighted Adamski-Type craft on October 8, 1953. This particular sighting was reported in the "EVENING NEWS" and stated that Potter was both an amateur astronomer and highly respected citizen of Norwich, England. Even Gene Duplantier in his Number Eleven issue of "SAUCERS SPACE AND SCIENCE" ran an article by Ronald W. J. Anstee in which he talked about space exploration and stated, "The reported conditions found by the sputniks and American satellites and now by 'Pioneer' are not new knowledge, the

Right: Official Brazilian Navy photo of dome craft. Below: Saucer photographed by Cedric Allingham.

Allingham says he took this picture of the Saucer on the ground.

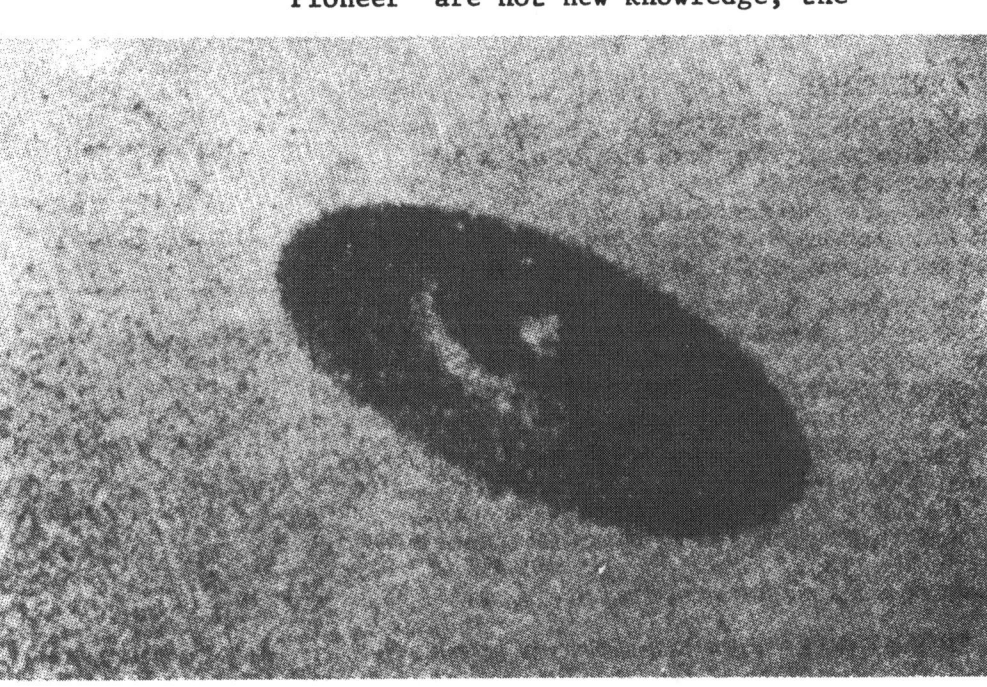

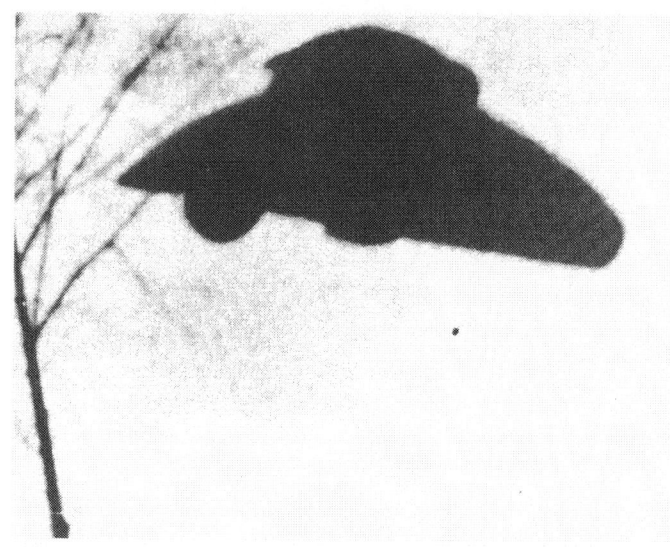

Single frame from movie of "Adamski-type" saucer shot by Mrs. Madelein Rodeffer. A strange effect which some researchers have termed a force field distorts image of craft on the right.

increased radiation activity and other conditions found in space, was reported several years ago by Mr. George Adamski."

It is plain to see that there is more than meets the eye in regard to the Adamski story and photographs. If they could have been faked who faked them? Anyone who has ever met George Adamski in person knows that he was a simple unimposing individual hardly capable of such an ingenious bit of photo fakery.

Who could set up a world wide conspiracy which could turned out photos and reports by the hundred to back and corroborate George's reports? Until these and other questions can be answered my mind remains open.

MORE ON THE ADAMSKI PHOTOGRAPHS
by Timothy Green Beckley

They say that a picture is worth a thousand words. But certainly in the case of George Adamski his pictures are worth ten thousand. These pictures, which adorn the text of his three major books, have stood the test of time and have never really been scientificaly refuted.

However some motion pictures (in full color) taken by Mr. Adamski which have not been seen very widely are perhaps even more sensational. In one case a very close associate of Adamski, a Madeline Rodeffer of the Washington, D. C. area, has an eight or nine minute film which she took in her back yard. These film clips clearly show the landing gear of a scout ship which is hovering between two trees. The landing gears are visible as the saucer tilts slightly to one side. One of those, a Mr. Harry M. Fleenor of Topeka, Kansas, who viewed the footage at Mrs. Rodeffer's home stepped off the distance in between these two trees and discovered that the ship must at least have been 75 feet in diameter. He also said that as he viewed the film he got a very eerie feeling, like something NOT OF THIS WORLD.

Certainly it is most easy to say that Adamski's pictures merely represent some chicken fencing, ping-pong balls (or a G-E Light Bulb if you wish) attached by a famous brand of glue. But even though admittedly such photos can be easily faked (and also easily discovered) this has never been the case with Adamski's photographs. In fact even if we are able to do away with his supposed trips to Saturn and other spots in space, and with a little imagination even his first desert contact, we have yet to find any really good explanation for his still and moving pictures. Certainly a photograph of any small model could be easily detected with little or no previous training in the field of photographic reproduction.

Perhaps Adamski was not telling all he knew or has clouded his story up by adding considerable pieces of fiction to it, yet I am convinced that somewhere in his stories lies a golden thread of TRUTH. Wheather he actually did all the things he claims (or was even the tool of some government or Silence Group) may perhaps never be fully discovered. But indeed his photographs are perhaps the best taken to date. Surely, at least in this

"ADAMSKI'S PHOTOS ARE REAL" researcher's mind, a complete re-examination of this case is in order. And up till we are able to discover the secret of his photographs there is certainly a good case FOR and not AGAINST George Adamski.

JERROLD E. BAKER'S STATEMENT

Not only did Adamski photograph saucers at Palomar Gardens, but a young assistant, Jerrold E. Baker, also snapped at least one picture.

The following statement, dated December 13, 1952, provides first hand outside evidence that the saucers, which Adamski photographed, actually did appear over Palomar. Following is Baker's sworn statement:

TO WHOM IT MAY CONCERN

During the time I was serving as an Instructor in the United States Air Force, it was my good fortune to learn of Professor George Adamski and the work he was accomplishing toward proof of the Flying Saucers' existence.

After being discharged from the Air Force on October 29, 1952, I came to California and began assisting the Professor in his work.

Last week was a very notable one because of a definite increase in the appearance of saucers. Midway in the week I suggested that we both spend some time in the morning scouting for them. I suggested that we both situate ourselves in two different places, he with the telescope and camera, and I with a Brownie. I learned that in photography this to be extremely important from my enlistment in the service. We noted that on Thursday and Friday the skies were filled with low flying military aircraft that continually circled the area as if searching or chasing airborne objects.

On Saturday morning, while I was sawing wood for the fireplace, the Professor called me and said that he saw what he thought to be a saucer coming over the coast. I hurried up the hill to the water pump and stood by a large tree. From there I could get a closer view of the coast but I saw no saucer. I looked towards the Microwave station in particular which stands high on the mountain almost due north, because the night before I pointed out to a young boy with me at the time a flying saucer hovering in its general direction. I thought perhaps this saucer might be headed in that direction and I didn't want to miss seeing it as has often been my experience by scanning in only one direction. For about ten minutes I watched and waited but nothing happened. Suddenly in the corner of my eyes, I saw a circular object skim over the treetops from the general direction of the area where the Professor was located. It was a flying saucer--of that I was sure. I seriously thought it was going to land in the small clearing because of its extremely low altitude. I waited momentarily mostly because of shock I guess as it continued coming closer. It then hung in the air not over twelve feet high at the most, and about twenty-five feet from where I was standing. It seemed as if it did this knowing I was there waiting to photograph it. I quickly snapped a picture and as I did it tilted slightly and zoomed upwards over the tree faster than anyone can almost imagine. I ran out from behind the tree hoping to catch another picture but I could only see a small object speeding towards Palomar Mountain--then it was gone completely.

Then in turning, I saw the Professor coming through the brush on the other side of the clearing and practically did flip-flops I was so excited over my good fortune. I had not for a moment dreamed he was able to photograph it through his telescope because it was so extremely low. But after he told me he had been successful in obtaining four shots, I persisted that we go to Carlsbad immediately. He agreed and I rolled

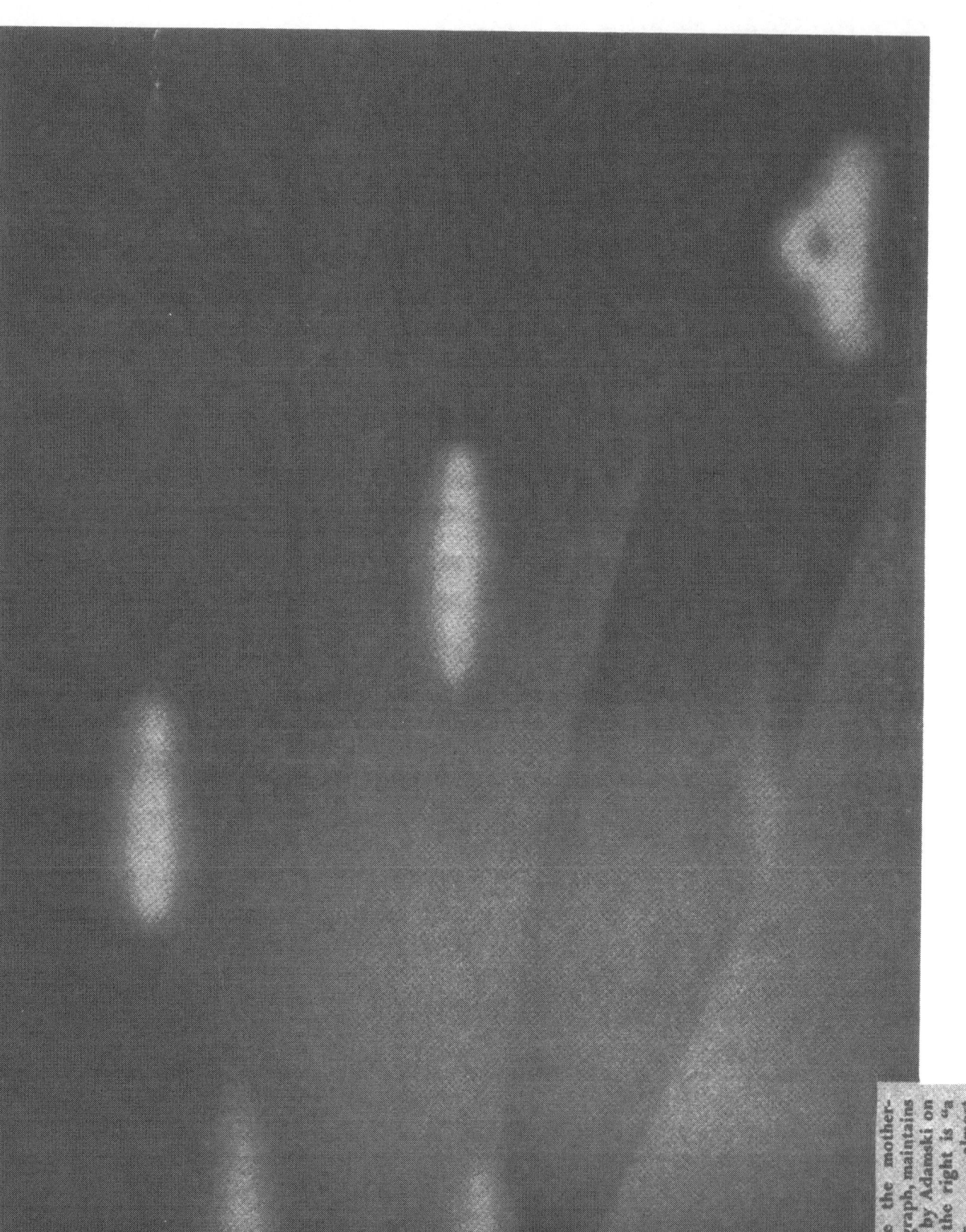

Flying saucers leave the mothership... This photograph, maintains the book, was taken by Adamski on March 5, 1951. On the right is "a similar giant carrier . . . almost identical to the one that brought the scout ship six months later." This was when the Venus visitor arrived the remaining portion of the film onto the exposed side.

Things happened so quickly that in the excitement of getting a picture I forgot many of the things I wanted to look for if ever I got close enough to a saucer. For I don't believe the saucer remained in my view for over two minutes.

These things I know for certain:

1. The saucer made no sound.
2. It was guided by superior intelligence.
3. There was a slight odor present as the saucer speed upwards.
4. It had portholes and three huge ball bearings presumably landing gears.

---Jerrold E. Baker

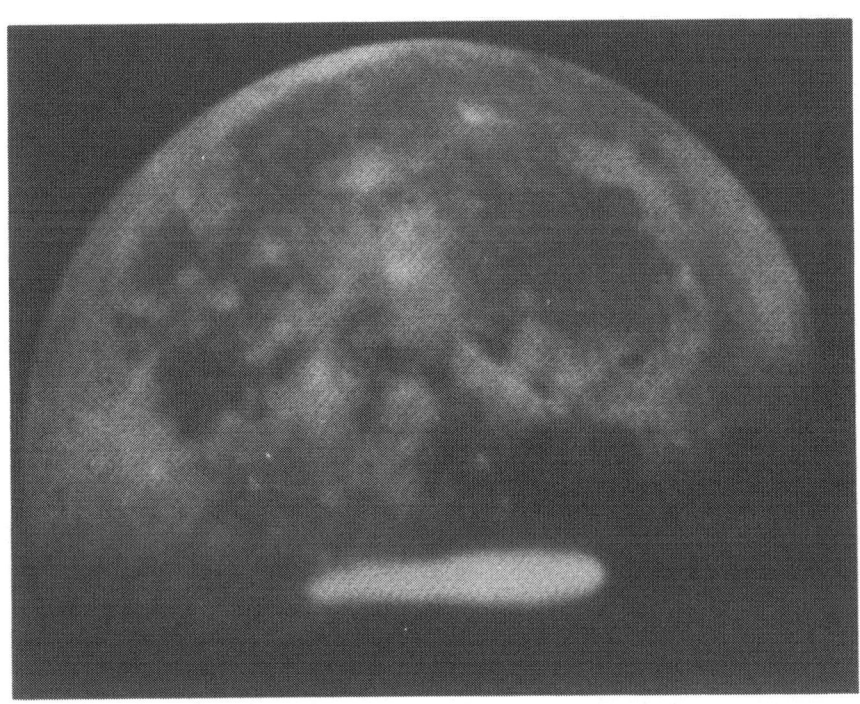

One of Adamski's telescopic photos showing UFO between camera and moon.

For list of available glossy photos of flying saucers, write to: Michael G. Mann, 140 East 2nd Street, Brooklyn 18, N. Y.

"Call us Silence Group if has to be. In silence we progress. Silence follows where we have gone. Our footsteps echo round planets when we march."
   -----Adonai Vasu

My Fight With The Silence Group

George Adamski

Throughout my public life in the promotion of the teachings of the Space Brothers, I have been visited by many agencies, including the F.B.I., Central Intelligence Agency, Air Force Intelligence, the U. S. State Department and people from other government agencies. Now I am not saying that these particular people tried to silence me. There are many facets of the Silence Group, and many of these I am afraid that neither I nor the general public know about.

What is and who is the Silence Group? There is likely an informal organization, that Keyhoe spoke about, and a formal organization which is more top secret than any of our intelligence departments.

During a recent trip to Washington, D. C. last year I learned that the Silence Group which is opposing the truth about flying saucers would like to see some kind of mystical religion spring up. Then they could say, "Didn't we tell you it was all mysticism, with the purpose of building up this religion, and there is no foundation of reality to it as we told you before?" In other words, they could then use this excuse to pigeon hole the entire subject of saucers. And I do know definitely that the men who came with the motive of hushing me were not space men. They were Earth men, born in this world and of this world.

It is odd that this silence Group does not bother anyone who is in the occult or psychic field. Such people can say what they want to say and have no one threatening or silencing them, as is done to them with concrete information.

They have even tried to distort my experience by referring to my former group in which I served as instructor on philosophy. The name of this organization was The Royal Order of Tibet, just as he said. But the order did not adhere to the teachings of mysticism as he implied. The lessons I gave in lecture form and many of them were broadcast over radio stations in Long Beach and Beverly Hills. I believe that if it were important, copies of these broadcasts could be obtained from the stations. These lessons consisted of purely philosophical talks on the laws of life from a universal concept which every person should know. But Ignorance leads to distortion.

Judging from my mail, Catholics, Protestants, Jews, Orientals, all religions and people from all walks of life are interested in and are supporting the thesis of space visitations from the physical, mechanical point of view, while few of them would be interested if it were thrown into the mysterious.

This is the factor the Silence Group knows to exist and fears. When the people of the world began thinking in accord on such a subject, the foundation of the money changers began to weaken. When people's eyes are turned upward, searching the skies for friendly space visitors, and their minds filled with longing for peace and happiness on Earth, it becomes difficult to fill their minds with hatred for their fellow men, wherein war finds a fertile field. And youthful minds filled with challenging thoughts of space travel are not easily diverted toward the rather questionable honor awaiting in bloody battlefields. Is this one of the things the financers see and fear?

It is because they fear the event which might bring peace and understanding among men of Earth, whereas war has become a financial investment that pays well for certain investors. Reports of personal contacts are being discussed by innumerable people of many languages and throughout the world.

This knowledge of interplanetary visitors who are friendly to Earth people, and who themselves have learned to live in peace with one another seems to have given new hopes to many who have lost hope, and a new purpose to life for untold numbers. It is this which those who control the purse strings of the world fear. Acceptance of the reality of interplanetary visitors would have far-reaching effects upon the present-day economic system of Earth. Everybody would be affected in a far greater degree. I believe they see this and are fighting it with everything they have, and at the same time endeavoring to remain conspiciously absent from the scene.

VISITED BY THREE MEN

Shortly after the publication of FLYING SAUCERS HAVE LANDED I was visited by three men, two of which I had met previously, but the third was a stranger. It was he who took the role of authority and direly threatened me, demanding certain papers I had, for one thing. Some of these I gave him, and was promised their return, but this promise was never kept. Since I I did not exactly understand to what he had reference, I did not give him some of my important papers. There is no need denying that I was frightened. Before they left I was told to stop talking or they would come after me, lock me up and throw the key away.

With these personal experiences to serve as a foundation, I wonder if Wall Street might be the central faction behind all the battling to keep the phenomenon of interplanetary visitation in the field of the occult, and combatting those of us who know and announce that the space people are physical beings, travelling in mechanical space craft. They would like nothing better than to have this whole thing thrown into the field of the psychic, called a cult, and discredited in the minds of sincere people throughout the world.

I still say, and I hope I am wrong, but indications seem to show that James Moseley and some others are tools in the hands of the group. For it takes money to do what they are doing. FLYING SAUCERS HAVE LANDED sold well, but I have received comparatively little from it. I cannot travel on my own and do the things they do, without sponsorship. So, in the case of Moseley and some others who is paying? Of course some

MY FIGHT WITH THE SILENCE GROUP

may be working themselves right into the hands of this Group, without knowing it, but surely some are fully aware of the whole picture, but know where their meal tickets are coming from.

Of course it could also be true---for I am sure that we on Earth here are not the poorest in the Universe--that there could be some influence of this sort coming from space. But so far as I am concerned -- and I receive mail from all parts of the world -- no evidence is showing up that could be interpreted to the effect that space men are trying to hush up people on this Earth.

If any hostile situation appears, as in some places it has, it seems to be a case of fear on the part of the Earthlings. For once in a state of fear, people can see almost anything, or can conceive almost anything. So I have not the slightest evidence that such has taken place, although there seems to be plenty of evidence that the powers of this world have their hands in it.

I was quite surprised to find the drawing showing faces peering from the portholes of the flying saucer I photographed at Palomar Gardens which appeared in THE SAUCERIAN.

I have heard the story that faces can be seen, upon examining the portholes in the photograph very carefully, since my book was first published. But try as I might, I have always failed to find those faces. However, I did get a passing glimpse of my friend's face as he dropped the message through the porthole to me. It is amazing how many faces can be seen there, according to reports, but upon later inquiry I was told by the space people that there was only the normal crew for that craft present, two people in it, the time they came over Palomar Gardens on December 13, 1953. Isn't it amazing what imagination can do for a person?

KARL HUNRATH

I now wish to discuss Karl Hunrath and Jerrold Baker, who were used as witnesses against the authenticity of my

Paul Rear, of Pasadena, Calif., thought he could see faces by gazing intently at the portholes of the saucer in one of Adamski's photograph. Rear's drawing above, printed in the Spring, 1955, SAUCERIAN, elicited much comment from readers, many of whom said they also saw the faces.

story and photographs in Moseley's January, 1955, issue of NEXUS.

You will recall that Hunrath, along with a man named Wilkenson, mysteriously disappeared in 1953, after claiming to be in contact with space people who were going to take them to another planet in a space ship.

I believe, incidentally, that Jerrold Baker knows where Hunrath is -- and that does not include another planet. According to the rumors that have persisted since his disappearance, Hunrath might be in Mexico, not far from the border. My reason for thinking Baker knows of his whereabouts is that about two years ago Baker and another man came up to see me one evening at Palomar Gardens. During the conversation which ensued Baker, showed me an ad cut from a newspaper which stated that anyone wishing to contact Hunrath should write to a certain post office box number. I neglected to obtain the name and date of the paper, however, for at the time I wasn't interested.

My knowledge of Hunrath goes back several years. When FATE magazine carried an article about my efforts to photograph space craft, along with some of my earlier photographs, I received mail from all over the nation, while people in all walks of life and from many places stopped in to visit me as part of their visit to the big observatory on top of Mt. Palomar. One of these visitors was from Wisconsin. He was a scientist and upon his return home, discussed the conversation he had with me with two of his associates, one of whom was Karl Hunrath.

Later Hunrath wrote to me personally, and we carried on quite an extensive correspondence. He seemed to have a fine scientific mind, and I enjoyed our correspondence. Later his letters developed that he seemed to be having troubles of one kind or another, losing one job after another, as he said, without a reason being given to him. Then I received a letter stating that he was on his way out to see me, and late in December, 1952, he arrived at Palomar Gardens, bag and baggage, with intentions to stay indefinitely, but no money to pay for his expenses.

Jerrold Baker had also arrived under similar circumstances, late one night in December, 1952. He was still there behaving as one of the family, helping himself to everything, freely and in abundance, but without money to pay for anything.

HUNRATH'S STRANGE MACHINE

A day or two after Hunrath had arrived he revealed to me that he had constructed a magnetic machine which he said would produce all the electrictiy we could use at Palomar Gardens (At that time we did not have outside electrical service, depended upon our own small power plant). He said he had left this machine in storage back in his home town, but would have it shipped to California. He would bury the machine in the side of the mountain where it could not be found easily. My curiosity and suspicions were instantly alerted, but not quickly satisfied. It took much careful questioning on my part to learn what I was seeking.

Finally, during a casual conversation on the subject, Hunrath volunteered that HIS MACHINE WOULD NOT ONLY ATTRACT THE SAUCERS, BUT WOULD BRING THEM DOWN!

Immediately it dawned on me that if it could bring down the saucers, it might be able to do the same to our planes, and many of them fly over Palomar daily. Asked about this point, Hunrath admitted that it might also bring down planes, and this is where I balked, telling him that in such a case we would be responsible for the lives lost.

To this he replied, "WHO CARES? WE WANT THE SAUCERS!"

I then forbade his bringing the machine to Palomar Gardens. That, of course, started the trouble which Baker is now carrying on. Up until then everything was fine, but when I told Hunrath that he would have to

MY FIGHT WITH THE SILENCE GROUP

move without further delay, Baker went with him. Yet within the hour before their leaving, Hunrath ordered me off my own property, adjoining Palomar Gardens, and for a few moments I thought he might attempt force to accomplish his order. Then he seemed to gain control of himself and left without further trouble.

I consider Hunrath's conduct unethical and his proposal unpatriotic, so I informed the FBI. These Government representatives agreed with my opinions, thanked me for calling them in. They took precautions that no physical retaliations would come to any of us at Palomar Gardens. Unfortunately they had no control over other avenues Baker would use in his attempt to damage me.

Rumor has it that when Wilkinson came from Wisconsin to California he brought Hunrath's machine with him. I have never tried to verify this, but it was shortly after their arrival in California that Hunrath and Wilkinson disappeared. If they are indeed across the border, they could have the machine there with them. I have been promised more information on this matter, but so far it has not been forthcoming.

If Moseley and others like him continue to use Baker in their attacks against me, let the barrage come. I am not afraid!

Meanwhile I shall still raise my small and perhaps inconsequential voice in an attempt to acquaint the people of the world with the true mission of the space people.

"I believe in
everything and nothing."
-----August C. Roberts

Questions and Answers

Most frequent questions answered by George Adamski

Quest. #1. How can I meet a space person and get a ride in one of their ships?

Ans. I honestly cannot answer this question. Nor, do I believe, can anyone else who has had experiences similar to mine. I am not able to arrange a personal meeting for anyone. I cannot do this even for myself! I am met when and where a meeting is to the advantage or convenience of the Brothers.

At all times, it is up to those from other worlds to identify themselves. However, I have been told contacts have been made in every nation , and with the leaders of every nation. Their coming and going is no secret to officialdom. This was reported in INSIDE THE SPACE SHIPS.

Furthermore, it is a fact untold numbers of Earth's inhabitants have met and even worked with the visitors without being aware of it. Unless some good can be accomplished, they do not identify themselves. With the restricting redtape many nations place on travel, such identification could be dangerous. That is why it is well to be skeptical of those who boast to their friends and fellow-workers that they are from another planet. An overwhelming majority of these people are impostors.

I can assure you of one thing: The space people are not coming merely to satisfy our personal curiosity. At the present time, I have been told, the best way we can help is by beginning to live with more respect toward one another. For as this is done throughour the world, fear and hostility between the peoples will diminish; leaving a fertile field in which to work for the betterment of all. But final success in this depends upon each individual.

Some scientists, I know, are receiving help from the space people; and many admit what they are "getting" is beyond anything before known or written in our present textbooks. Still, much information must be witheld.

We have much growing to do before it will be safe for us to be given a full understanding of the natural forces that they have harnessed for propelling their ships. For this same energy can be perverted for terrible destruction as easily as it can be used for the progress of mankind. We must learn to live humbly, respecting our fellow man regardless of his color of skin or position in life. But this is a problem each person, and each nation, must solve individually.

Quest. #2.   Why are SAUCER sightings concentrated in so-called "flaps"?

Ans. According to the Brothers, there was a plan being formulated by certain governments to tell their people all UFO's seen during these past years were mainly our own and Russian satellites, and natural phenomena. This obviously would have been only another attempt to discredit the reality of visitors from other planets, but it nevertheless would have raised many doubts in the mind of a questioning public.

So intermittently thousands of space ships are brought here to put on a public display over periods of two or three days. Such "flaps" receive wide publicity in the press, while isolated sightings no longer receive much attention. While the Brothers do not wish to make mass landings at this time, they want to prepare the minds of people all over the world to accept them as reality. With such concentrations of space ships the public can no longer doubt that there is something to "flying saucers."

Quest. #3. Are the space people coming to save us?

Ans. No! Some people are fostering an erroneous idea that the space people are here to save a "chosen few" in the event of nuclear warfare, or if a disaster should strike. This is totally false. Should they be in the vicinity when a catastrophe is taking place, they would do their utmost to help if possible; but they are not actually coming our way to save us from conditions into which we have placed ourselves. Each planet, each individual, must fulfill its own destiny by solving its own problems.

The law of brotherhood has been handed down to us through countless ages. They live this law. So were they to save any peoples, it would not be just a "chosen few." It would be all within reach. They would not discriminate. Remember, they do not recognize our racial or religious divisions.

Quest. #4. Have space people helped Earth's inhabitants in any way thus far?

Ans. Yes. They have helped us in many ways of which we are little aware. To cite but a few: Any of the small conflicts that have plagued the world in recent years could have developed into world-wide destructive wars had it not been for their efforts. And the cold war which has continued for so long could have flared into open hot war had they not intervened in different ways and places.

Besides, they have done much to neutralize the radio-active conditions created in our atmosphere through our bomb testing. Were it not for their assistance in this, radiation would be much more prevalent than it is today As time passes, the public will become cognizant of many other ways in which they are helping.

Quest. #5. What are the green fireballs that are sometimes accompanied by explosions?

Ans. Fireballs are not new. They are as old as Nature herself, for they are a natural phenomenon often seen during and after an electrical storm. They are, in fact, all concentrations of electrical energy; and as a natur-

QUESTIONS AND ANSWERS

al force are beneficial to life on a planet.

However, as a result of our nuclear tests, a false and dangerous condition has been created in our atmosphere. At times these concentrations of radiation will gather together and, while usually invisible, under certain conditions can extract enough elements from the atmosphere to appear as "fireballs." With their finer instruments, space people are able to detect these false fireballs or pockets of radiation. visible or invisible; and when they do they intercept and disintegrate them with a higher frequency ray. This is but another of their ways of aiding us.

In the case of both the natural and artificial fireballs, when the concentration of energy becomes too intense toward the center, an explosion comparable to spontaneous combustion takes place. This explains some of the sonic booms that have been recorded when no jet planes were in the vicinity; and also accounts for the erroneous reports of "exploding" space ships.

These fireballs have been seen and reported in several different colors; and the most frequent being green. Remember, however, space ships themselves can on occasions closely resemble a fireball when, in certain maneuvers and at certain speeds, they glow green, red, orange, white, ect. One is often mistaken for the other.

Quest. #6. Can you explain the disappearance of some of our planes?

Ans. We all know what an atomic cloud looks like after the explosion. That cloud is really a concentrated mass of energy. As it travels around the world, it keeps transmuting itself towards an invisible state as it drops the debris picked up by the explosion. And it will continue in this state indefinitely.

These clouds are composed of the same concentrated energy as the "false fireballs" mentioned in the perceeding question; only on a much vaster scale. Compared to the phenomenon discussed before, these concentrations are enormous. It is such a "cloud" that is responsible for many plane disappearances, for it is in a higher state of concentrated, activated energy than when it was first released. Since it is invisible, a pilot is unaware of its existence.

Should one of our planes contact such an invisible "cloud," it would either explode or disintegrate, seeming to disappear before the eyes of the onlooker. This explains some of the mysterious plane disappearances that have been reported. Since on several occasions space ships were being tracked on radar, and in some instances even visual reports were made of them in the vicinity of a disappearing plane, the implication has been that space ships were kidnapping our planes.

But I have been told, that because of our inefficient instruments for detection, space people know our pilots are helpless in the path of these "clouds." To avoid these very tragedies, they do their utmost to reach the concentrated mass as quickly as possible.

However, there have been occasions when they arrived just as one or more of our planes were entering one of these pockets of concentrated energy. Under the circumstances, they were unable to do more than stand by; because once a plane is caught in such a force it is impossible to save either the plane or its occupants. But they then later disintegrate the invisible cloud to avoid further catastrophe.

Quest. #7. Why do astronomers say atmospheric conditions around our neighboring planets is such that human beings like us could not live there?

Ans. First of all, I know of no astronomer who has actually traveled to another planet to learn whether or not the atmosphere around it is similar to ours. So how can they be sure? Theory, yes! But as scientific developements progresses, theories are constantly being replaced by facts that prove many theories wrong.

For example: Not many centuries ago astronomers worked from the premise the earth was square and flat, and there were only seven planets in our solar system. But as science advanced and better instruments were developed, we located other planets; and by circumnavigation proved the world to be round.

While the spectroscope works well within a given distance, are we sure it works efficiently between planets? It is my belief that no instrument we now have is capable of accurately reading conditions immediately surrounding another planet. Studying conditions in space could be compared with trying to photograph an object a long distance from the camera, through a large body of water. For space is comparable to an immense "ocean" with its waves of energy and every-changing "space debris."

Quest. #8. Is there air on the moon?
Ans. Yes. Our scientists know that in order for any form to retain its shape, the inside and outside pressures must be equal. Atmosphere surrounding a body in space furnishes the pressure necessary to keep that form from exploding or disintegrating. Enormous pressure are built up within all planets, yet the atmosphere surrounding them offsets this by exerting a perfect balance of pressure from without.

Being a smaller body, the moon has a comparatively lighter atmosphere; yet not so light that human beings from earth and other planets could not acclimate themselves. For have we not observed the man-made bridges, the tunnels, and the space craft bases on the moon in recent times?

Furthermore, if our scientists and government officials were not sure that atmosphere surrounds the moon, they would not be expanding so much money, time, and effort to reach our natural satellite. They know, as do you and I, that it would be impractical to carry sufficient oxygen in ships to make living on the moon comfortable for those who land there. And if, as they are saying, the first nation to reach the moon will control the destiny of Earth's inhabitants, they must be counting on enough natural atmosphere to enable the construction of primary installations from which operations could be carried out. Consider, too, that not only will oxygen be needed for men's breathing, but for the operation of all equipment. For no motor, not even atomic, can run in the absence of oxygen.

Again let me remind you, there are people living on the moon in peace and happiness. If any of our nations hope to reach this body and land there, plans should include peace and friendliness toward those whose home they will be visiting.

Quest. #9. Was the asteroid belt between Mars and Jupiter caused by a planet exploding as some believe?

Ans. No. The space visitors have told me the asteroid belt is not an exploded planet nor is it, as has sometimes been stated, one destroyed by "evil forces." Rather, it is a natural incubator within which, according to natural law, planets are born to replace the present worlds as gradually disintergrate, Other bodies necessary for the perfect balancing of the system are also created therein.

This belt serves the purpose of a vibrator or agitator, agitating what

QUESTIONS AND ANSWERS

we call the "still" force into an active force. This is essential to all systems. For the asteroid belt is actually electro-magnetically charged. Each minute particle is individualized and illumined with the natural energy contained within its particular area, and is growing or disintergrating in an ever-changing relationship. Were it not for this belt of intensified activity---and two more farther out---our system would not have the necessary power to maintain its existence. For a clearer understanding, these belts can be compared to the action of what we call the armature of a motor. But the natural energy thus created is without amperage; and serves the system somewhat as a booster station.

The particles in an asteroid belt are in constant collision. Sometimes this results in a blending of the two, creating a larger body; sometimes in an explosion, exactly like crossing two hot wires of electricity. Similar belts without number exist throughout the Cosmos. All serve as generators or agitators of energy, as well ss promoters of it. The necessary reaction to create energy, which supports all bodies within itself, is brought about through this constant friction.

To some this may appear as a conflict in the Divine Plan. But it is not conflict as we know it, where one is set against another for destruction. Actually, it is construction; comparable to the conflict between a male and female in the field of reproducing young. It is an orderly conflict in which one phase lends itself to another for the common good of all.

This is the explanation the space people gave me regarding the purpose of the asteroid belts. I pass it on in an effort to clarify this mystery in the minds of those seeking a greater understanding of the universe in which we all live. As we build ships and travel space, we will learn from experience the truth of this and other information given to us by those who have already attained this knowledge through their own experiences.

While on the point of the origin of this asteroid belt, let me quote from one of our scientists, Dr. Arthur M. Harding. In his book "ASTRONOMY, The Splendor of the Heavens Brought Down to Earth," Page 129, Dr. Harding writes, "it was at one time thought that perhaps the planetoids resulted from the explosion of a single planet which once revolved around the sun between the orbits of Mars and Jupiter. It can be shown, however, from a study of their orbits that they could not have resulted from a single explosion."

His discussion of the planetoids while short, is very interesting and enlightening.

Quest. 10. Does the often discussed "tilt of the Earth" mean total destruction?

Ans. No, actually, only a small portion of the planet will be directly affected. In these days of rapid world-wide communication systems, any catastrophe can be minimized. Our foremost scientists are studying this movement closely, and a ample warning of danger will be given.

This tilt is not the result of our firing the huge bombs, nor is it punishment for "the sins of the world." It is a natural, orderly change which occurs to all planetary bodies. Nature is constant motion; constantly changing, yet adhering to definite time cycles which cannot be altered by Man. So the tilt of the Earth, bringing up rested, fertile land from beneath the seas to replace worn-out ground, is but fulfilling a Cosmic time schedule. Were it not for these "rest periods" for depleted ground, no planet could continue to support life. A portion of land, which in some long ago cycle was withdrawn from man's use, will rise. While other lands will again be covered with life-giving seas to be revitalized; to someday, in a far distant cycle, rise again for man to use. This has happened countless times in the past, so you can see our "world" is not going to be destroyed.

From above, where their vantage point gives a greater overall observation, and with their technical knowledge and more advanced instruments than any on Earth, the Brothers are watching, too. When findings are definite they will gladly share them with us. How much this could mean to us depends on how receptive we are when the time comes.

Should these warnings from our scientists and the Brothers be ignored, as has often happened in the past, there will be great toll of life. However, if people will but realize that with life they can rebuild and again accumulate the possessions they hold dear, the toll of life can be minimized. But survival will depend upon heeding the warning to leave for safer parts. Here again, is an individual problem; a decision each must make for himself.

Quest. #11. Do you support what is commonly known as psychism or mystic channels?

Ans. I do not disapprove of any field of exploration, nor the attempt to develop any form of human ability. For even out of false promotion, the truth will eventually emerge. Misuse of the Law is usually brought about through ignorance.

There is a vast difference between true Law, which is never possessive and caters to no one, and the so-called "laws" which glorify the personal ego. God, or the Divine Creator, is a respecter of no person, nor is Nature, His creation.

Delving into psychic matters is a dangerous pastime without first acquiring a thorough knowledge of one's self, one's relation to the Cosmos, and the factors with which one is dealing. For lack of this basic preparation, Man in his searching has followed many avenues which have led only to confusion.

There are no "short-cuts" to true development. Yet, working with patience, in time man can attain access to Cosmic knowledge. Psychism and mysticism, as improperly understood and practiced, can lead only to bewilderment and often danger.

Quest. #12. What is your opinion of messages received through the Ouija board and automatic writing?
Ans. Again this goes back to lack of understanding of one's self and a relationship to the All. Under a form of self hypnotism, one usually tunes into the first level of impressions, which is the earth itself. Since there are 2½ billion minds in this world, the first impression level thus contacted would produce representative "messages"; thought forms of greed, fear, hatred, divisions, self-aggrendizement, forecasts — and always the low-grade pranksters.

Truly divine messages threaten no one, judge none, and never create fear. Such messages never contain personal predictions. Using this rule as a yardstick, it is reasonably easy to determine whether what is received is stemming from a low level of this world, or is Cosmic in nature. Again, we do not deny the Law; we merely deplore misuse of the Law through lack of understanding.

Quest. #13. Do space people materialize and dematerialize?
Ans. No, they do not! If they were capable of materializing and dematerializing, why have they bothered to build metal ships? This necessitates the mining, smelting and alloying of the metals, building the space ships and manning them with crews. If they possessed the mystical powers of materialization and dematerialization some on Earth have accredited to them, all this would be a needless waste of time and effort.

We know from tracking their ships on radar, and from examining them after they have crashed, that they are indeed very "material." I can-

QUESTIONS AND ANSWERS

not stress this point too strongly. They are normal human beings of flesh and blood the same as we on Earth.

Quest. #14. Where can one learn the Universal Laws and how to use them?
Ans. My course on Telepathy explains these laws as I have used them, and as the Brothers tell me they are used by the people on our neighboring planets. These are not the normally accepted teachings on telepathy, but in them I explain what a person is, how he operates, and his purpose for being. This understanding is essential for the unfolding of true telepathy. For there is no truer saying than, "Man know thyself and all things shall be revealed unto you." All nature is simple; so are the Universal Laws.

The Universal Laws are not new or unknown to Earth's people. They have been handed down for countless centuries through our philosophical teachings. But because to the average person these teachings have been cloaked in mystery and relegated to the field of the abstract, few people recognize the kernels of Truth lost amidst the mountains of chaff. We must remember, True Philosophy is nothing more than the science of living according to the purpose for which all forms were brought into being. There must be eternal growth and blending; but never divisions.

To return to telepathy. I have been asked if a person reading this will be able to contact the space people. This I cannot promise. Development and success depends entirely upon each person's application of the information given. Already, with the little given in INSIDE THE SPACE SHIPS on telepathy, a number of young people are having remarkable success in mentally communicating with their friends. This I believe, is a very good illustration of the proverb about learning by becoming "as a little child." For their minds are not yet cluttered with the preconceived ideas their elders have unquestioningly accepted as concrete facts. And in many minds, these "concrete facts" offer a barrier which precludes the entrance of any new concept that is foreign to their preconceived ideas.

Quest. #15. Can space people receive a thought from any of us today?
Ans. Yes, they constantly do. As fully explained in my book, INSIDE THE SPACE SHIPS, it was in this manner that a certain group of space people tested and proved my sincerity, then chose me as one through whom they could speak to the peoples of the world.

They are also aware of many others who are sending thoughts their way, and in many instances they do respond. But, I am told, most people have kept their minds so occupied with sending out thoughts concerned with a contact, that any chance of establishing a "receiving station" was impossible. Obviously, unless the telepathy can work both ways, contact cannot be completed.

To people of all ages who are interested in telepathic contact with our space visitors, I always suggest they test themselves with Earthly friends, both for sending and for receiving thoughts. For if a man cannot receive mental messages from someone with whom he is already acquainted, how can he expect success with those from other planets?

Quest. #16. Do you believe in reincarnation?
Ans. Call it what you will, obviously there is a continuation of life. Life is eternal, and eternity means without beginning and or ending. You have been, and you will continue to be, whether in this world or in other material worlds.

Divine Nature knows no waste. Proof is to be found in the study of any of her aspects. The tree matures to giant stature through centuries, only to eventually crash to earth and crumble into dust. But this very dust fertilizes future trees so that they, too, can grow straight and strong. So it is with the "lives" of a human creature. Each life experience, when rightfully used, adds strength and understanding to future lives yet to come.

Would it not be sinful waste for man to be created only once, placed without reason in the position he now occupies in the world -- then be consigned by a capricious Creator to what we call heaven or hell for eternity? This would be neither logic nor progress, and the Law of Progression is the foundation of the Cosmos.

And as the Brothers have explained to me, that which we call spirit could not manifest if it were not for material form through which to express; nor could the material exist if it were not for the spirit, or Cause. So Man, whether or this world or others, after laying down, or moving out of the material body he has been using, does take on another through which to express and learn from experience.

Quest. #17. When we have learned our lesson in this world, where do we go next?

Ans. If this question means which planet -- no man knows! But all planets are school rooms in the Cosmos. And just as we graduate from grade to grade in our school system, retaining and using knowledge learned in the lower grades, so we graduate from planet to planet and system to system. The Cosmos is a vast school with many departments of learning for every state of being. There are primary planets, and planets advanced far beyond the scope of our earthly imaginations. But we are eligible, eventually, for all. What we need to concern ourselves with here, is to try to master the lessons of the present that we may the more speedily inherit the future that is surely our destiny.

Quest: #18. If what you say is a fact, where then are heaven and hell?

Ans. These two terms have reference to states of conciousness rather than to definite locales. It has been our misinterpretation of reality that has led us to be taught that heaven and hell are actual places, located somewhere out in the vast Cosmos beyone the earth. Today many people are living in hell right here, because of the confusions, uncertainties and divisions; all of which creates fear, want and hatred. Yet our planet, being the handiwork of the Creator, is a divine creation.

When one understands himself, his purpose for being, and his relationship to the All, he rises in consciousness to a heavenly state of naturalness wherein, because of his understanding of creation and himself, he has compassion for all. This does not mean a state of blissful unconcern. On the contrary, people who have attained the understanding are actively interested in all that goes on about them. Criticism from others does not disturb them, because they know that others are learning lessons just as they are, and this constant growth and development will continue throughout eternity. Nor do they condemn another for what today might be considered a shortcoming, because they recognize these very "short-comings" as by lessons to be learned. Thus they do not label one act as good and another as evil; but look upon the whole as an unfolding through experiences.

At first, this idea may not be acceptable to those who have never thought along this broader line. But a careful look around will convince us of the truth of these facts. Some people enjoy dancing; others think it a sin. Who is right? Each person is firmly convinced he is! One person enjoys serving his fellowman in every possible way; another prefers to be served. Is one right and the other wrong? Who is to say?

The wise man does not judge. He looks upon the whole as the working out of the Divine Plan, knowing full well the Creator does not condemn, does not find fault with any segment of His creation.

Living in peace with one's

QUESTIONS AND ANSWERS

fellowman is but a matter of understanding and compassion. It is a Universal Law we all must learn and apply in our daily contacts with others if we are to progress.

Quest. #19. Are all the space people vegetarians?

Ans. No. During the year 1958, I had the pleasure of attending a meeting comprised of people from Mars, Venus, Saturn, Jupiter, Uranus and Neptune, It was a friendly get-to-gether, devoted mainly to discussions of some of our everyday problems. The subject of eating was introduced, and I asked for more specific information, since so many questions regarding this topic are coming to me.

Their answer was simple and precise. On their planets they do not raise cattle for slaughter. They eat fish at about the same ratio most of us eat meat, while their meat eating is comparitive to the average earthling's fish consumption.

They have studied our food carefully, and in view of present conditions on earth find they are healthier if they eat meat approximately once or twice a week while here. They told me they usually purchase the cheaper cuts which can be boiled with vegetables, much like my mother used to cook when I was a boy. They are very fond of all vegetables, and make appetizing soups from beans, potatoes. ect. Raw fruits and vegetables prepared as salads are greatly enjoyed by these people. Of course they continue to eat fresh fish whenever obtainable.

In other words, they pointed out they are not fanatics. Those worried about the consumption of any particular food might do well to heed the words of Jesus: "Not that which goeth into the mouth defileth a man; but that which cometh out of the mouth, this defileth a man." Matt. 15:11.

Quest. #20. Have you ever heard of Ashtar? (Applies to Monka of Mars and other entities coming through mental channels)

Ans. Yes, Many times. From all I have been able to learn, "Ashtar" communicates only through mystic channels. He claims to be commander over several million space men, and makes promises, prophecies the future, speaks of good and evil, threatens, divides, etc., none of which conforms with what I have learned from the space people. I have never had Ashtar's existence as a physical space traveler corroborated by those with whom I meet.

A number of Ashtar "messages" have been sent to me, and upon reading them carefully I have found bits of truth scattered here and there. But this is always the case; for falseness could not exist if it were not for the real from which it is patterned. It is the presence of these little bits of truth that causes to so much confusion in the minds of those who sincerely seek reality, but who want it on a factual rather than a mystical basis. If anything is universal, it will blend but not divide.

While I do not deny the existence of people on planets beyond our system who are both higher and very much lower than ourselves in development, why should we follow "guidance" from anyone who cannot help us? With our present distrustful attitude toward one another, surely we do not need to reach out into space to add to our divisions.

I could admit the actuality of Ashtar as a thought vibration, much in line with thoughts from the past and present civilizations of earth, but nothing more. Such thoughts can be picked up by anyone who opens his mind to the reception of whatever might be passing. That is why we should at all times be selective regarding the impressions we entertain.

Quest. #21. Do the space people use money as a medium of exchange on other planets?

Ans. No. Their means of exchange is a commodity and service exchange system, without the use of money.

"For what shall it profit a man, if he shall gain the whole world, and lose his own soul?"
-----St. Mark 8:36

Space Age Philosophy

George Adamski

POSITIVE & NEGATIVE THINKING

Many people have undertaken the study of positive thinking during the last few years. In many ways positive thinking is just as bad as negative thinking. Either one of these is an extreme. A middle ground exists which is desirable and beneficial to use and seems to be generally overlooked.

An example of the dangers of positive thinking was Adolph Hitler. He used it to an extreme and became power crazy, distorting his whole program through use of this type thinking. On the other hand the masses were negative thinking. They too, when they began to act, became victims of negative thinking carried to extremes.

What is the correct way of thinking if both of these methods are bad? The catalyst that produces correct thinking is motive. When we say correct thinking, we do not necessarily mean good thinking. Instead it is a balanced thinking using two forces, positive and negative, and introducing an effect called motive. Many different types of motive exist. Motives may harm people or they may help them.

The particular law involving motive operates through every avenue of human expression and behavorism. A motive for self-betterment, excluding all others, cannot bring anything but bad results. It is the separation of ones self from all others which promotes undesired selfishness and glorifies the individual ego.

A motive to help as many others as possible automatically elevates or betters the avenue through which it is promoted. Example: If I am to promote good will in my neighborhood, I will do everything in behalf of the world's population, not including and forgetting myself. I do not need to include myself since I will be the avenue through which the betterment will be expressed. I am automatically in it. This kind of good and motive is Cosmically recognized.

The personal desire for self betterment is like the positive thinking without the negative support. It is bound to bring forth confusion and finally total disatisfaction, unbalancing the person. It makes little difference if it is positive or negative it will do the same thing. If one's motive towards self-betterment is positive only or negative only, experience will bring forth half-truth only, regardless of the actual motive, for one part of the unit has been left out. To be perfectly plain it is a dangerous practice.

To be successful in a self-betterment program one must become a servant to the many as stated before, then the "many" helps them to develop or fulfill the motive of their desire. All this is according to divine plan. In so doing the ones whom we help in this endeavor automatically become our teachers. This because no two minds are alike; each mind you are trying to help renders some reward to you for the effort you are making in understanding that mind. In truth you actually teach each other. This is the true motive of life, as well as the true method of self-development.

Christ made it very plain; if you come in through any other door you are a thief and robber. To us a thief and a robber do not lead pleasant lives, yet they may be happy in their own environment. This is not the happiness of a natural state for one may be happy, though ragged and dirty provided he is in the company of the same. One cannot be happy, regardless of how they strive for it, nor can they learn the higher laws of life and the Cosmos by serving only the few. Blessed are they who do the Father's will, serving all creation of which they are an integral part.

To fully understand one's self, one must serve the untold numbers. As untold numbers exist there are untold avenues of divine expression. No single avenue nor the few can serve the understanding of one's self, anymore than the sun which shines upon us all, could suddenly withdraw and shine upon one form only. This would not be fulfilling its purpose. The motive should be through the "many if one is to "know thyself." A good example of this is my own experience.

Since I have the desire or motive to help millions to the exclusion of myself, I have been reborn a dozen times in the undertaking of this service. Some of the births were unpleasant while others were very pleasant, according to our judgement. The birth was given to me through the many whom I have served, for not one failed to teach me something.

Each one of the thousands and thousands of letters I have answered taught me something worth much more than the money, gold, or all the fame this world can bestow. That which I learned through the letters gave me new birth and made me the man I am. Continous answering of these letters will bring forth another man of me tomorrow. The greater the numbers I serve in my small way, the bigger the man they make of me, as through them I better understand myself. If I were to serve the few or myself alone, who would teach me the things I am to know? The knowledge of myself would be as small as the numbers I had served.

My advice to you is: Serve as many as you can, the greater the number you serve, the greater will be the understanding of yourself. This really should be the motive of everyone who desires to fulfill the destiny for which he was born.

Does not God serve all creations? He has no thought for Himself. This is why He is supreme and unless we, His children, do likewise, we shall not be abiding by His will. Let me ask this question: Does God ask a reward for supplying us or any of His creatures, their daily needs? No, He does not. His rewards will come without being asked when His creation fulfills the purpose for which it was created. So it should be with man. This is the only motive that will fulfill man's purpose on earth. It has worked so well on the other planets.

MANY ARE CALLED BUT FEW ARE CHOSEN

Since man of earth lives as a dual person; expressing more of the effects of the world, which is the mind; and less of the Cosmic, which is the soul; he finds himself in his present state

MANY ARE CALLED BUT FEW ARE CHOSEN

of confusion. This is especially true when he follows the traditions and conventions created by the mind for ages, that are as false as the mind itself. Fear, the governing factor, gives the individual soul very little chance to express itself.

All life depends upon the cosmos for survival, and its rewards have been "supply." Man, on the other hand, looks to men for his supply and as a result fear governs his life through experiences of want and disease. The soul keeps crying out service unto the divine Father, for it knows the Father; the mind, service unto itself, for it has never seen the Father. Tradition has taught it to fear that which it does not know.

While all are called to fulfill the purpose for which they were created, few choose to serve. Even these few seldom go through to the complete fulfillment of their destiny. The faith it takes is not of the heart but mostly of the mind. The evidence is present, for the mind demands credit for everything it does. If it does not receive it, it reverts back to the traditional and conventional way of life where it feels its security lies. In other words, it has faith in man but not in God, yet the Divine Father is the giver of all things, not man. So man goes on earning his so-called "security" by the sweat of his brow, a slave to other minds like himself.

When the "Brothers" came, during the most dangerous time of our lives when annihilation threatened us all, many responded. Sad to say, few are left. Many reverted back to the rewards and security of this world, prostituting the finest jewel ever placed in the hand of man.

Even those who professed a "revelation" from Christ in these darkened days have strayed away for the glory of the mind and the security through that lash of the whip-- The will of the mind. This, to such an extent, that those of us who stick to the original purpose cannot get the help needed to carry on.

So again we may say, the teachings of the Divine Father, through the "Brothers," has been sold for the gold of this world and the satisfaction of the temporal mind.

During my 71 years of life I have not gathered the things earth considers as wealth, but I have never been in want. The supply was there which is greater than any wealth or security on earth. This wealth I will carry thru eternity; this is my security. I have unshakable faith in the Father who gave me birth; not once has He neglected me, nor shall He as long as I serve his purpose to the best of my ability. He has never disappointed me while other human minds brought nothing but disappointments.

You may say: But God helps those who help themselves. That too is a perversion, used to defend the sense mind. The real meaning is God helps those who helps themselves to His will. Thy will be done, not mine, is the true meaning. May I ask one question of those who claimed to have received a revelation from Christ before undertaking this work? If this be true, how could you give it up for earthly rewards or other opinions? There is no greater truth than this kind of revelation for it is given by Cosmic Consciousness.

HOW TO KNOW A SPACEMAN IF YOU SEE ONE

This is to answer the many inquiries in regard to this question. It is not an easy question to answer as the people of other planets are images of the same Creator as we, and look no different than we do.

When it comes to knowledge they are far ahead of us in relationship to things in the cosmos that we still have to learn. Only by talking to them can one tell if they are of this or another world. Even then it is hard to make a decision since we are learning so much about space. Unless one has understanding and is truthful to himself and his Creator, interested in the welfare and betterment of people in this world, he could easily be fooled. Here is an example:

One evening while living on the mountain (Mount Palomar) we heard a light knock on the door as we sat around the dinner table (it was raining very hard at the time). When we opened the door a tall fine looking man stood there asking for me. He looked no different than any other earthman. He was asked to come in and sit with us at the table. No car was in sight, how he arrived I do not know. His opening question was the type anyone would ask and from there we proceeded with space discussions that went on for at least an hour. From his conversation we concluded he was not an earthman, for some answers he gave could not have been read in any earth literature about space.

Towards the middle of the conversation I felt he was definitely a spaceman, however others present later expressed doubt. At a recent meeting with the "Brothers" I met this same man and learned he was in charge of the schedules on which ships from Saturn arrive. He reminded me of that evening and this is what he said:

"The reason you identified me at that time was not so much from what I said but because your soul and your mind were as one and it was your soul that recognized my soul. This was consciousness recognizing consciousness and not the mind recognizing the mind. the others present judged me with their minds and questioned my identity and purpose, thus failing to blend with my soul for the truth they wanted. Some always ask for spoken verification which will never be given. If we say who we are they will not believe it. We are not permitted to identify ourselves in the manner which you people are expecting, by saying we are spacemen from so and so. Intelligent people would not accept that, and we would only be satisfying the curiosity of the ego. This we are not here to do.

"Others ask for miracles; magicians can perform those. Only one answer exists to the recognition question. That is a blend of consciousness as you did with me that evening, for in consciousness we find truth and not in the mind.

"As for taking people for a ride in our ships, that is desired from a curiosity standpoint rather than a sincere desire for knowledge of the truth. This is of no value for the service which we need. Only

Cosmic Consciousness. You know that is required for a pleasant journey, yet how many do you find who are willing to blend their consciousness with all - consciousness? Not many, for this involves a sacrifice of one's personality or ego (sense mind) unto the dictates of consciousness where the mind is servant unto its Creator. It cannot be unto itself as it is in your society.

"You have had an example of that in your own group, individuals asking for personal contacts and instructions from us before they will go on working for the betterment of mankind. They should learn to blend their soul consciousness with the Cosmic Consciousness. You did it by faith as we do; every time we take a trip to your planet we must have faith, for many hazards exist in space. Without faith truth shall never be known. The mind that has no faith shall never know true life or happiness. Consciousness is the real man and not the mind. Consciousness is the father and mother of all things including the mind. When the mortal mind tries to operate only in behalf of itself, it is opposing the Supreme Consciousness.

The Supreme Consciousness knows no fear, as does the mortal mind, for where there is truth there is no fear and the only truth there is---is in consciousness.

"Anyone who wishes to be of help to us will have to learn, at least to a small degree, to blend their soul consciousness with the Over-Soul of the cosmos. Then they may recognize us when we meet. Many from earth have already met us unknowingly."

So, my friends, you now have the answer as given directly by a space person. Do not forget, for you cannot learn this by yourself without instruction.

ANNIHILATION

If we stop and take a good look at the way most humans behave, we question whether or not they are ever going to progress. As there are parasites in most kingdoms of life, so there are in the humans as well. They may appear to be well behaved and intelligent in their endeavors of life, but it is restricted to a narrow field of their own. Their endeavor, if well examined, is very personal, 90% of their acts for personal gratification. This is far from Cosmic Purpose.

Would we want to see people go on who for ages have not changed one iota, but have caused nothing but misfortune and misery for the majority of others? Or, the men of war and those who spread false rumors, never finishing anything they start?

All nature, abiding by the Cosmic Plan, deals with all creation on an even keel and leaves no unfinished business. From this we should learn the ways of everlasting life for nature is everlasting. It is a constant state of change but never deviates from the plan. Nature always eliminates that which fails to serve its purpose.

A man was given two arms for a purpose, but should he fasten one to his body and never use it, it would soon wither away to such an extent it would never be of service to him.

Did not nature eliminate certain species when they no longer served the Cosmic purpose? It is no different with man.

Two types of thinking exist on this. The man who calls himself an athiest or agnostic will tell you that when you are through in this world you are through forever. Another will insist that life continues. Both of these are right for if such potential were not present we could not think of either one, for thoughts are things. To have life everlasting--one must earn it. That is the reason Jesus said: "The tree that bears no fruit is cut down and consumed in the fire and is no more." He also cursed the fig tree for bearing no fruit, menaing that everything should render service unto its creator, and not take the glory of its form unto itself as so many humans do.

To be plain, all forms must serve the purpose for which they were created if they are to continue. Did not Jesus also say: "Fear not the one who slays the body but fear the one who slays the soul. Some religions, like the Hindu, teach that if a man fails to serve the purpose for which he was created, he may return, not as a man but as an animal, reptile or vegetable. This is the same as a tree consumed by fire; it will never be a tree again. Part of it was released as gases in smoke; part of it remained as ashes before the wind and will be used again, but not reproducing the tree as it was. This is also true of the man who fails to identify himself with the Cosmic Plan. His elements (the atoms of his body) will keep on serving in other fields but he as an ego will never exist again.

The ego is the personality or carnality. That is why it states in the Bible, carnality is born to die. It can die one kind of death or another but it must die. One form of death would be unto itself by becoming a humble servant unto divine plan. In this way it earns a life of eternity. Like a drop of water, if it stays by itself and serves its own purpose, in time it will evaporate and never return as the same drop of water. On the other hand, if this same drop of water unites with the ocean it would lose its identity as an individual drop of water (or meet death as to its individuality); yet it actually would gain life eternal, keeping its experiences as an individual drop and uniting them with experiences of the ocean. This continuing as long as the ocean remained in existence. If it had not done so it would have a very short life and experience as a drop of water and then evaporate in non-existence.

You can see here how a man is a composition of two souls, just like the drop of water had life which was the soul of it, which originally belonged to the soul of the ocean. When it returned to the ocean it was like the prodigal son returning back home, through humility once again uniting with the household. The drop that remained as a drop acted as an independent soul, which we call "personal." It did not come anywhere near the ocean, let alone into it, and governed itself according to its own selfish desires. It displayed its independence as a separate thing from all others. It was concerned about itself and its own welfare and as a result composed a lot of fears, fro it could not help but feel something bigger than itself unto which it was in subjection. Since that part is the parent of it, it caused the drop to remain in a constant state of indecision, not knowing if it should step into the

unknown and lose its identity as an ego or remain as it was and evaporate with no future.

This is the meaning of "not my will but thine be done." If my will remains as it is, it will have an ending as it had a beginning. Since the ocean has no visible beginning or ending, any drop of water united with it will have the same and would be alive today and forever.

So it is with man, unless his will becomes one with Cosmic Will

ANNIHILATION

he will have an ending as he had a beginning. That you might better understand I will analyze three cases that came to my attention.

CASE NUMBER 1. This particular lady has been confined to her bed for fifteen years. During this time she has gradually lost her memory of earthly experiences. Today she does not recognize her own sister and she can feel no pain. Her body is in perfect condition except it is gradually turning into a jelly-like form, an indication of disolving. The substance of the body is returning to its original state which is gases and carbon. If this will continue until nothing but bones remain is yet to be seen. There is no doubt that this person has been dying for fifteen years in memory, which must have been quite unpleasant at the beginning. Today she is all dead except the body.

This a good indication of annihilation, since memory is the only thing of the ego that is to carry on after death. This person will never again know herself as the same person or entity. The forces that are at present controlling the body are cosmic or Universal and will continue on when the body fully dies, as they do now without her mind. This is the Cosmic Soul which will build another form to work through, but without the same ego the body represents at the moment. Why did this happen?

CASE NUMBER 2. This individual's interest was 80% in the earthly and 20% in the Cosmic. Now he is dying in the 80% of his memories. For days he remembers nothing and recognizing no one, yet every now and then he becomes fully alert as he was known to be, recognizing those about him. This person is going to have a second chance for he has given enough thought to the cosmic principles during his life to blend himself with the Cosmos. It is this force of life that every now and then awakens his memory. This means some of his memory will be carried over which will remain as an identity in the Cosmos. Even in this second chance during another lifetime he could still annihilate this identity if he did not improve upon the 20%.

CASE NUMBER 3. I knew this man personally. He had become so interested in human kind that anything that would happen to humanity would hurt him, for he took all creation as a Cosmic manifestation. For days he would sit by himself and gaze into space. He definitely was blended with the Cosmos and from that point of view you might call him a holy man. There was one thing wrong. He lost all memory of earthly activities thereby dying to the earthly life and living only the Cosmic. Yet the purpose of the Cosmic and earthly is to blend together for one is cause and the other, effect.

The only time there will be perfection is when there is a perfect equilibrium between the two. This means that he will have to come back to some earthly life to balance up, for there will be no extremes in the Cosmos. He will have life eternal, for he already has that without his earthly identity.

When Jesus said "temperance in all things," whether it be in earth or in heaven, he showed that balance is the law. So, now taking the Cosmos into consideration in our lives is bad, but the same is true if we do not take the earthly life into consideration also. Both of these must be lived as one, if one is to have life eternal with identity.

One can observe the law in action for invisible space is a part of the earth and earth is a part of space. Because there is a balance between them they manifest as one. One could not continue without the other. So it is with man.

"The parade of evidence in regard to FLYING SAUCERS HAVE LANDED could go on almost indefinitely.

-----James W. Moseley

Moon Probes Confirm Adamski's Claims

Adamski's books usually drew only two different reactions from readers. They either believed he was sincere and that he was telling the truth -- or they reacted quite violently and angrily, denouncing him as a fake. While utter belief in any document, without proof is certainly not a mature reaction, the scorn of Adamski's critics was much more imature.

Many of them, unable to prove Adamski wrong, predicted that United States and Russian rocket probes would completely refute his books.

The probes, however, very early in the game began to upset these critics and cause them some embarrassment.

For example, John Glenn's description of "fireflies," seen during his orbital flight, tallied with a similar statement made by Adamski in 1955.

The following report, uncovered by researcher, Timothy Green Beckley, is taken from a publication of limited circulation issued by New Zealand Scientific Space Research   We quote it verbatim:

In February, 1966, LUNA 9, made a successful soft-landing on the Moon. An equally successful feat was performed by the SURVEYOR on June 2, -- The findings of both space craft have since been published and in all fairness to the late George Adamski, who published his description of Moon conditions through the medium of his book, INSIDE THE SPACE SHIPS, in 1955, we would do well to compare notes.

On Page 144, English edition (Page 160 American Edition) of INSIDE THE SPACE SHIPS, Adamski, while viewing the moon from a distance of 40,000 miles through a special instrument,

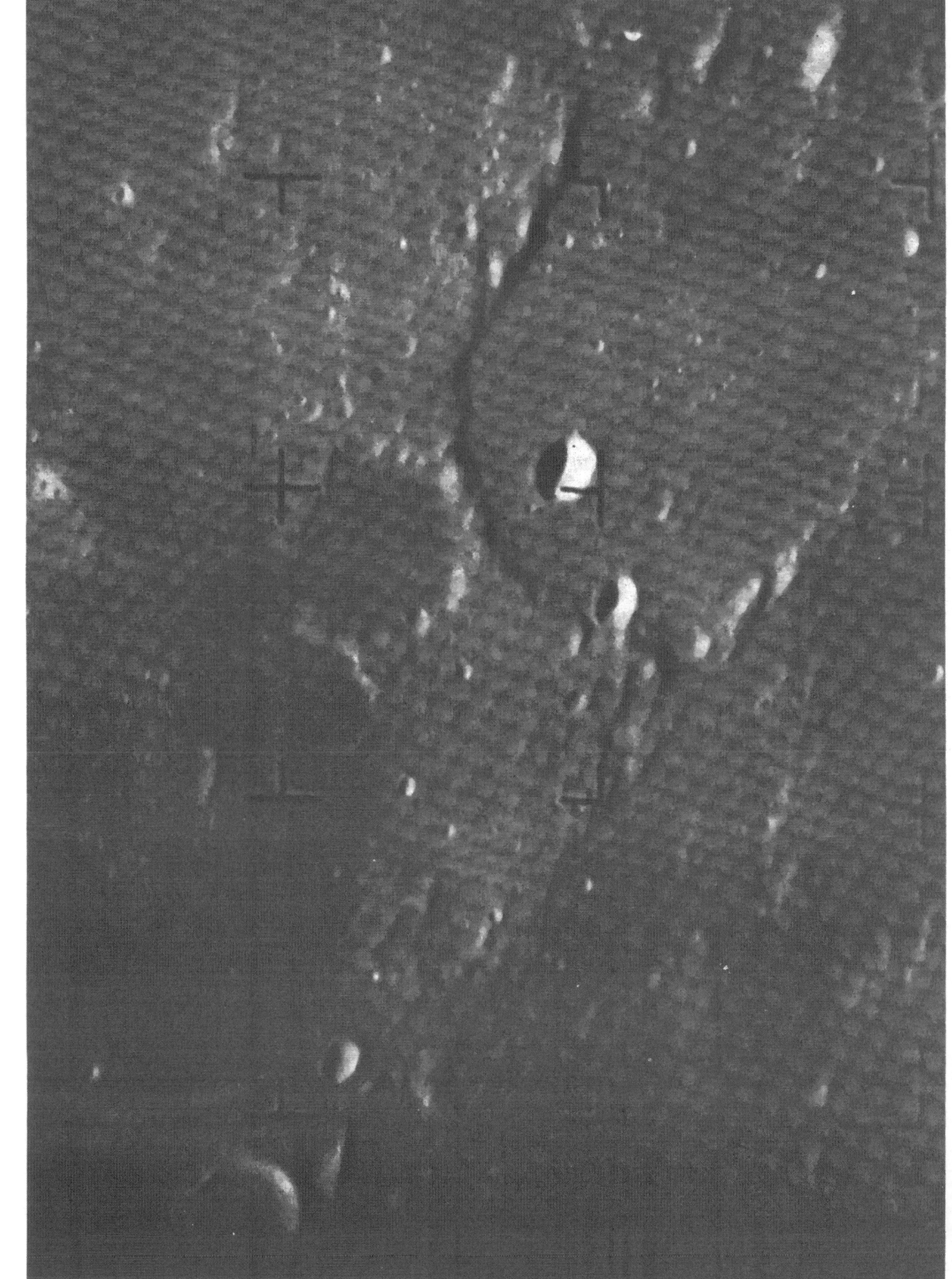

Ranger photos, such as one below, tend to confirm Adamski's claims.

continues: "I noticed deep ruts through the ground and in some of the imbedded rock, which could have been made in no other way than by a heavy run-off of water in times past. In some of these places there was still a very small growth of vegetation perceptible. Part of the surface looked fine and powdery, while other portions appeared to consist of larger particles similar to coarse sand or fine gravel."

"Many of the craters are actually large valleys, surrounded with rugged mountains, created by some past terrific upheaval within the body of the Moon." He goes on to say: "True, some of the craters had been formed by meteorites hitting the Moon's surface, but in every such case, these craters showed definite funnel bottoms."

In the Science section of TIME MAGAZINE, February 11, 1966, there is the following report regarding findings of LUNA 9:

"Taken by a camera with a wide-angle lens from about ten feet above a porous, pumicelike surface, the pictures showed a barren, forbidding crust, littered with jaggard rocks and tiny pebbles that the Russians later revealed were as small as one or two millimeters wide." The TIME report continues, quoting University of Arizona Astronomer Gerald Kuiper: "The surface of the Ocean of Storms seemed to have been formed by lava flow during volcanic activity billions of years ago."

In the N. Z. HERALD, June 3rd, 1966, we find the following regarding the area in which the SURVEYOR landed:

"The terrain surrounding the spacecraft appeared somewhat like a rocky beach with small objects scattered on the surface. No small craters were immediately apparent and the surface appeared reasonably smooth and hard." One Scientist of the Jet Propulsion Laboratory said: "It looks like they have prepared a landing field for us."

Comparing our present-day with descriptions given by Adamski, In 1955, we cannot but conclude that Adamski knew what he was talking about.

"The flying saucer mystery
is a masterpiece of
organized confusion."

-----Dominick C. Lucchesi

The Strange Case Of R. E. Straith

Gray Barker

I remember very well the very cold day in February, 1958, when I went to the post office, expecting to receive the usual mail.

The usual mail was there: Approved contracts from film companies, advertising proofs on a movie publicity campaign, a letter from a woman in Idaho explaining how three creatures had landed near her barn in a strange soup bowl with legs---and a number of subscriptions for THE SAUCERIAN BULLETIN, which I was then yet publishing.

I had opened this mail first, and although I found it more interesting than usual, I was saving until last a large Manila envelope which I had signed for at the Certified Mail window.

The main point of interest was the return address: George Adamski, Palomar Terrace, Star Route, Valley Center, California. I had corresponded with Adamski from time to time, but he had never before sent a large envelope marked "Photo, Please DO NOT CREASE."

What I withdrew from the envelope was more startling than any UFO photo that I could have widly expected. It was a photostat of a document that completely amazed me. It would cause world-wide controversy and draw comment from the staid London Times. It would cost me sleepless nights while I underwent investigation by the F.B.I. It would lead to a campaign of slander and perscution.

Now turn the page, and read, as I first read on that cold February morning, a most unusual letter, ostensibly from the U. S. State Department!

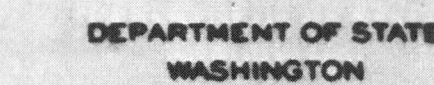

DEPARTMENT OF STATE
WASHINGTON

Prof. George Adamski
Star Route,
Valley Center
California

My Dear Professor:

For the time being, let us consider this a personal letter and not to be construed as an official communication of the Department. I speak on behalf of only a part of our people here in regard to the controversial matter of the UFO, but I might add that my group has been outspoken in its criticism of official policy.

We have also criticized the self-assumed role of our Air Force in usurping the role of chief investigating agency on the UFO. Your own experiences will lead you to know already that the Department has done its own research and has been able to arrive at a number of sound conclusions. It will no doubt please you to know that the Department has on file a great deal of confirmatory evidence bearing out your own claims, which, as both of us must realize, are controversial, and have been disputed generally.

While certainly the Department cannot publicly confirm your experiences, it can, I believe, with propriety, encourage your work and your communication of what you sincerely believe should be told to our American public.

In the event you are in Washington, I do hope that you will stop by for an informal talk. I expect to be away from Washington during the most of February, but should return by the last week in that month.

Sincerely,

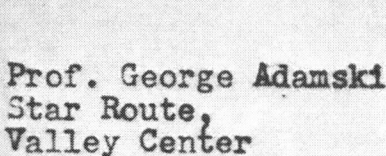

R. E. Straith
Cultural Exchange Committee

RES/me

EXHIBIT I

Exhibit I (Continued): Reproduction of envelope which enclosed the "Straith Letter," reproduced on opposite page. Reproduction has been reduced slightly in size to fit page.

As a publisher of a flying saucer periodical, my first thought was the great opportunity to "scoop" the field. I published a rather small bulletin which was quick to get to press and into the mail. I almost ran back to the office with the thought of getting a special issue underway.

As I ran panting up the steps to the office, I began to have misgivings.

Could the letter be real? Was the government ready at last to admit the existence of flying saucers? Was it taking this means of releasing the information?

Or was it a slip? A mistake of some sort?

I sat down and examined the letter carefully. Although, in photostat form, the letter could not be proved to be on Government stationery, I trusted Adamski too much to think that he could have made a paste-up of some kind and had it photographed.

Should I publish the letter after all?

It did seem to be private correspondence, as the first paragraph pointed out. The writer stated it was not official.

At best I feared that it was written by some over-zealous employee who would really be put onto the carpet if the letter were publicized.

Also I began to fear that I might suffer repercussion from the State Department if I published it. Instead I decided to forego the scoop take a more conservative course, and publish only the letter Adamski had written to accompany the photostat. A reproduction of the actual letter follows:

GEORGE ADAMSKI
Advisor

EXHIBIT II (handwritten)

COSMIC SCIENCE

EXHIBIT II (handwritten)

STAR ROUTE

VALLEY CENTER, CALIFORNIA   Febraury 17, 1958

Dear Mr. Barker:

Although it has been a long time since I have received your bulletins, I know you are kept busy with them and other work. I am sending you this information because I believe you will be interested in it and able to use it well.

As you can see from the date on the envelope, the original letter was mailed on December 16th. I hesitated releasing it because I did not want to cause any trouble for Mr. Straith. Yet the letter was of no value until released. So I investigated in every way possible to be sure of who Mr. Staith was and of whether or not he would be hurt.

The time has now come for the people of our nation to know of the contents of his letter and to act, if they want the truth of our interplanetary visitors, which could also lead into paths of peace and interplanetary scientific development rather than destruction which is now staring us in the face.

Therefore I am asking you and everyone I know to get this information to the people in every way possible and without unnecessary delay.

From unimpeachable sources I have learned that the Air Force is in no poisiton to give such information to the people. It is a subordinate department of service in our government whose leaders are appointed and can be released from duty by orders from one person higher up. Only from Congress can such information come. And from the contents of the accompanying photostat letter we learn that the State Department, through its own researches, does have the facts.

The members of Congress are elected by the people As their representatives, each such representative owes a responsibility to the people who put him in office. And it is these men alone who are in a position to give this truth to the people of our nation and to the world.

Booklet #2 of Questions and Answers will arrive from the printers next week. In it is a copy of this letter. And with it in mailing will be a letter asking the people to write to Vice President Nixon, their senators and their representatives in the House demanding that they release the facts which they have available to them regarding the space travelers. Since these men look to the votes of the people to keep them in office, I am asking the people to tell their representatives that unless the truth that is so badly wanted and needed is forthcoming within the near future, they need not look for support and reelection in coming elections. Pres. Eisenhower is not eligible for reelection.

As I have been told, the people, according to our Constitution, have it in their hands to be given the truth. They have now been told how to get it. So it is up to them to prove whether or not they are sincerely interested in the matter, suggiciently to act. For if Washington is flooded with letters, telegrams, telephone calls and visitors demanding this one thing, results will be forthcoming quickly.

Mr. Straith experienced quite a battle within himself before writing that letter. He knew what could be its results, and the many possibilities facing himself and many others if the people of our nation were not wholeheartedly sincere in their attempts to have authoritative information revealed. And to have complete success there must be prompt and united effort from every part of our nation.

Photostats have been sent to many nations and the people there are but waiting word from here to give it public release. I am sending it from here to all who have expressed any interest in the matter. And I am asking the support of every group I know to get the word around. I can do no more. But this will prove how well the American people can stand together and work as one toward the accomplishment of a goal vitally important to the entire world, but without monetary recompense, at least at present, to anyone.

With best wishes to you always,

Sincerely,

George Adamski

GA:lm

After deciding on this middle course I wrote suggesting that it might not be wise to release the letter, since it might be breaking a personal trust on the part of its writer.

Adamski replied, on March 21, 1958.

"I was somewhat surprised at your apparent attitude.....implying that I was betraying a trust. This, I have never done. Please reread the third paragraph of Mr. Straith's letter of which you have a photostat.

"Quote: 'While certainly the Department cannot publicly confirm your experiences, it can, I believe, with propriety, encourage your work and your communication of what you sincerely believe should be told to our American public.' Unquote.

"How else could this paragraph be interperted except that I share this information with the public? Had he said he was writing only to encourage me, asking me to keep it confidential, I assure you no one would have heard of the letter.

"As for the authenticity of the letter, I wonder how many people know that the Seal of State, impressed just above the salutation of the letter, and clearly visible in the photostat, is never impressed until _after_ a letter is written and signed. This Seal is highly guarded and only certain people are permitted the privilege of using it.*

"Another angle that seems so strstrange in this entire matter, is the fact that at times the official attitude has been that the craft moving through our atmosphere, and being sighted over every nation, are _not_ of this world. Then, a short time later, they will refute their own statement. Yet, in spite of every effort there remains an interesting percentage that cannot be explained except as coming from out of this world. Furthermore, from time to time government officials have publicly stated their belief in these interplanetary craft. Why, then do even those who staunchly support the reality of these craft continue to frown upon admitting the actuality of personal contacts with the people manning these ships!

"..... I have been told that the government of Brazil and Venezuela have officially admitted that certain sightings in their countries were 'not of Earth aircraft.' I have also been told that Russia is investigating public interest in this subject, and is about ready to release authoritative information on it." **

---

*Whether or not the seal is impressed only after a letter is written has been subject to some controversy and was never directly cleared up by the State Department. A letter from Maurice S. Rice, Chief, Public Service Division, State Department, of September 3, 1959, and addressed to George C. Wilson, however, states:

"I am unable to respond to your request that this reply be written on stationery of the same kind as the letter which Mr. Adamski received. The white-seal blue-embossed paper is used for correspondence _signed by the Secretary and Under Secretary of State._"
(Underlining ours--G.B.)

My reluctance to 'scoop' the saucer press by publishing the letter was apparently inadvised. For a British rival, THE FLYING SAUCER REVIEW, came out with the letter in their next issue.

Meanwhile excitement broke in London.

**Russia did not release "Authoritative" information on UFO's, but some few years later Russian Scientists released opinions that: (1) The Great Siberian "Meteor" of 1897 was no meteor but likely an atomic explosion caused by a space ship blowing up; (2) The moons of Mars were hollow; (3) the Biblical cities of Sodom and Gomorrah may have been destroyed by atomic explosions!

Desmond Leslie, co-author of FLYING SAUCERS HAVE LANDED summoned reporters to his London flat and distributed copies of the letter. The Times, usually ultra-conservative, felt disposed to run a 12 inch story about it, complete with a run-down of Adamski's contact with the Venusian.

John Pitt, a personal friend of mine, and an editor of the leading British spiritualist newspaper, PSYCHIC NEWS, air-mailed me the clippings, along with the results of an investigation he had personally made.

Although I knew that he had long been a critic of Adamski's claims, I did not doubt the veracity of his information

THE UNITED STATES GOVERNMENT HAD JUST DENIED THE AUTHENTICITY OF THE STRAITH LETTER!

Apparently the Times story had stirred up quite a hornet's nest, with various representatives of the press hounding the American Embassy. Pitt quoted me the official statement, which had just arrived in London from Washington:

"The American Embassy has received a number inquiries concerning a purported Department of State Letter, photostats of which were made available at a London press conference Wednesday. A check with Washington on a copy of the photostat supplied to the Embassy has resulted in the following information:

"1. We have no record of any person by the name ever having been connected with this department.

"2. There is no division or branch of the Department of State with the title 'Cultural Exchange Committee.'*

---
*Although there officially was no department so named, there was, at that time, a "cultural exchange" program involving the United States and the Soviet Union, and this of course, was administered by the State Department -- G.B.

"3. The department is looking into the matter to investigate the possibility of misuse of official department letterheads."

Pitt gave me a further rundown on his investigation. The Press Relations Officer at the embassy had told him that the layout of the letter did not conform with carefully detailed instructions that are issued to State Department employees on how letters should be composed.

For one thing, the letter was written on embossed stationery---a type used only for top-level inter-departmental correspondence --never to members of the public. The letter had not been mailed in the normal manner, that of franking, but put into a mail box in the city of Washington.

In an article for PSYCHIC NEWS, a clipping of which Pitt enclosed, he further added, "There was something hopelessly wrong with the signature. It was not written in the simple, slapdash, effortless scrawl that people use who sign many letters. It was far too studied, had variations in its slope, and had clearly been drawn with obvious care by somebody who had never written that signature before in his or her life."*

This was an entirely new developement. I had never thought about a hoax. I read Pitt's material, sat down and tried to figure it out.

But if the letter were indeed a hoax, WHY?

Who wrote it?

For what purpose?

Adamski?

Even if he could have, by some unimiganable method, obtained offic-

---
*See signature comparisons later in this section.

THE STRANGE CASE OF R. E. STRAITH

ial stationery and written a letter to himself, this would have been an obviously-unwise move. For the letter would have been immediately denounced, and Adamski would have known that. The letter could discredit Adamski, perhaps ruin his reputation. Adamski as the author was thus ruled out.

Was the letter, written by some unknown person, a diabolical plot to deliberately discredit Adamski?

According to Pitt, the letter obviously departed from the format used by such official letters -- so much so that it seemed that the writer was making it EASY for the letter to be "exposed." If a hoax, did the writer INTEND for it to be denied, and written so that such a denial would be immediately believed? Such an exposure would not only cause more confusion about the reality of saucers, but would create disbelief in Adamski's teaching, and tend to make the entire field of civilian saucer research a thing to be taken as a giant joke.

I picked up the telephone and placed a person to person call to a "Mr. Straith" in Washington, D. C., telling the operator there would likely be few Straith's listed. As I feared, there were NONE listed. Whoever had written the letter had been very thorough to pick a name that did not appear in the Washington directory (unless listed).

My statement in my June 15, 1958, SAUCERIAN BULLETIN, summed up some of my thoughts at the moment. I said:
"The three men who visited Albert K. Bender would seem to be Government agents of some sort, but when you think it out clearly, you can't quite believe that. Do there exist agencies of an almost supra-governmental nature, which because of their secrecy, are not known about generally: Or are there some sort of private 'Silence Groups' functioning with some evil and unknown purpose? If such an agency, or agencies are functioning, they have done their job very well They have created organized confusion. Some, who really knew, were silenced, perhaps, by other means."

The end of this section would perhaps be the best place to sum up my theories as to the genesis of the Straith Letter. But the paragraph above still contains, to my belief, the best explanation. And the paragraph that follows cannot be completely be ignored:

"The three men (still quoting from my 6/15/58 BULLETIN), however spooky they be in their dramatic black garb, are, after all, much easier to deal with than the less-tangible but even more diabolical techniques, such as the Straith letter may well represent. For these intangible demons can be dealt with only by the careful exercise of human logic and the human heart. In facing such a combatant bear in mind that you are facing logic that does not always follow a logical pattern---almost as if you were dealing with some alien intelligence that does not think in tereestrial terms...."

Are we suggesting that a Space Man wrote the Straith Letter?

Hardly, but nobody will probably ever know!

For myself, the first rumbling of a damaging and very frightening chain of circumstances began to occur.

Within a few days an investigator from the State Department showed up at my office.

I explained to him that I was only reporting news and showed him the photostats of the letter and the proof that it had already been published before I, myself, had ran the letter in the BULLETIN.

The investigator, however, did

not seem to be there to protest my finally publishing the letter (as I nervously suspected when he arrived) but instead wanted names of people publishing saucer magazines. He asked various questions about the saucer field in general. He said he was attached to the Pittsburgh office and that he investigated routine matters, mainly qualifications of people who applied for jobs in the State Department. Although I have never checked this out, I have my doubts that the State Department had such a division in Pittsburgh.

Meanwhile the 'saucer grapevine' was rattling with a very uncomfortable rumor. This rumor had it that Donald E. Keyhoe, director of NICAP, privately (so that no libel action could be taken) was spreading the story that I had written the letter.

I spent many hours pondering the NICAP rumor. I knew that Keyhoe didn't like me because of what seemed to be an obsession with him about so-called "contactees," -- or people who claim to contact and talk with space people   I knew that NICAP held to a preconceived idea that all "contactees" were liars. Although NICAP believed that saucers came from space, its directors seemed to exhibit an almost neurotic hate against "contactees." I had consistently held the editorial columns of the SAUCERIAN open to claims of all sorts, and all sides of every story   I had the feeling I was not liked by the Washington group because of my open-mindedness.

There was also an uncomfortable rumor going around that NICAP was NOT a private organization as it claimed, but a quasi-government group, financed secretly by the Air Force, CIA, or some other branch   Former military men were on the Board of Governers, including the former head of the CIA, Vice Adm. Roscoe H. Hillenkoeter.

The possibility entered my mind that NICAP, if it indeed was a military or intelligence front, could be behind the letter itself and trying to "frame" some other party! But I dismissed that as too fantastic   I knew they would like to discredit Adamski's claims, but somehow I just couldn't believe they would go that far.

I thought of other people in UFO research who might be connected with it if indeed it were a hoax, as the State Department investigator had claimed.

There was James Moseley, whom I didn't get along with well, mainly because he continually wrote unfavorable articles about people who allegedly contacted space people and had published some articles against Adamski in his magazine, SAUCER NEWS. I still couldn't figure how he could have obtained the stationery unless he, as some rumored, was really doing secret work of some sort -- some said for the CIA, others for the Air Force. I knew he didn't have to work for a living. And this was indeed puzzling.

On a hunch that I might find some clue, I dug out his correspondence folder and began reading some of his short notes to me, and my replies.

Something about one of my own long letters to Jim seemed to fascinate me. I don't know how far I read into it when I began to slow down and to do a very violent double-take!

A cold chill came over me, and I confess that at that moment I could almost see iron bars closing in around me.

"MY GOD." I <u>HAVE</u> BEEN FRAMED," I shouted out loud.

I arose from my hunched position at the file cabinet and sat down at the desk, while I began to inventory the serious situation.

I placed the photostat of the Straith letter beside the carbon of my own letter to Jim in the hope that

THE STRANGE CASE OF R. E. STRAITH

I had made a terrible mistake--but I hadn't.

BOTH LETTERS WERE OF IDENTICAL TYPE STYLE. THE STRAITH LETTER HAD NOT ONE SINGLE INDENTATION, neither for address, complimentary close, etc. Whoever had typed the Straith letter, HAD TYPED IT IN EXACTLY THE SAME FORMAT STYLE I HAD USED FOR YEARS.

I wondered who to go to for help. A lawyer? As soon as possible. A typewriter expert? I knew of none near.

I opened some of my mail from that morning that had gone unread because of my concern with the Straith matter. In it was the November, 1958, Special Bulletin from NICAP.

"Justice Department Hunting 'Straith' Hoaxter," one of the back page stories read.

Not only had a letter been received by Adamski, the article went on to say, but an officer of the Civilian Saucer Intelligence of New York had also received a similar communication, apparently written on the same typewriter!

Lonzo Dove, NICAP member and amateur astronomer, had loaned the Government several letters "written to him on the same typewriter, and signed by the supposed hoaxter, a man well known in UFO investigation."

My concern even deepened. I knew that I had corresponded lengthly with Dove, while I was using the same typewriter on which I had written the letter to Moseley.

Was Dove in on this thing too? I sincerely doubted this. I knew he was anti-Adamski, but I had always found him a very sincere, straight-forward individual who would not maliciously damage anybody.

I called a lawyer whom I had known through a civil case and briefly outlined the circumstances.

"It looks as if the FBI will be there to investigate you," he told me, "if the story in the NICAP circular is correct. You know the Justice Department is the same as the FBI."

His advice boiled down to two alternatives.

"Come in and see me day after tomorrow. I'll be out of town tomorrow and I can't see you now. Meanwhile here's my advice. If any investigator visits you in the meantime, here's what you should do. They probably won't have any search warrant at this stage in the matter, so if you are mixed up in this, show them NOTHING and tell them nothing. Tell them you have to get the advice of your attorney. If you're NOT guilty, you have nothing to hide, so tell them anything they want to know and show them anything they want to see!"

"I have nothing to hide," I replied, "So I'll work with them in any way possible. After all I too want to see the bottom of this thing gotten at!"

I had no opportunity to consult with the lawyer further, for in the forenoon of the next day two FBI investigators from the local area came to visit me.

They confirmed the Keyhoe claim that the CSI of New York had received a similar letter, though they said it was not written on any official stationery. They said it obviously was written to one officer to discredit another officer, since it contained snide remarks about the other. It was signed only by a short first name, "Kip."

The investigators, as had the State Department man, asked me who I thought might have perpetrated the hoax, and I had no definite ideas.

Then the comparison of the typing came up and I gave them complete details on this situation.

Prior to opening my own office,

I had done my desk work in the office of a part-time employer. This office contained two Remington standard office typewriters of the manual type. I had used one of these machines fairly constantly, and had also done all of my personal correspondence on it, along with occasional use of the other machine. Both machines had the same type size and face, the same as had been used to type the Straith letter. I had typed all of my old SAUCERIAN magazines on the one machine. This had been prior to 1954. In that year I had opened my own office, purchased one Royal typewriter and had been given a used IBM machine.

The Remington I had used was still owned by the same people I had worked for though the other Remington (which I had used infrequently) had been traded in. I urged that they get a sample of the typing from both machines and have an expert compare the type samples with the Straith letter, for the one machine was quickly accessible, and the other, although it had been disposed of before the Straith letter had been written still likely could be traced and examined.

I now felt somewhat better, for the FBI agents had treated me very courteously. I had been so shaky, however, I could not remember all of the details they gave me. For example, they mentioned another letter, evidently a spurious letter allegedly written by Keyhoe to the FBI, or vice versa. I would like to know more about this.

Anyhow, I had told them the truth and I had offered any assistance I could give them. I still didn't think it possible, in this free contry of ours, for an innocent man to be framed.

I decided to intensify my own investigation. One of my first actions was to call up my trusted friend, Alex Mebane, one of the officers of CSI.

He confirmed that he had received the letter which the FBI had described. Though it was not written on any letterhead, the sheet contained a spread-eagle watermark about three inches in diameter. He promised to send me a photostat (see Exhibit 3) though the entire middle of the letter, which contained the remarks about another member, were folded under when he made the copy, evidently for personal reasons. The references to "Wanda" and the National Science Foundation were completely meaningless, though Lex added jokingly that he wished the latter references were true!

Then he revealed another development. Apparently letters were flying in all directions! Coral Lorenzen, head of Aerial Phenomena Research Organization (APRO) had also received a letter, similar to the one he had, in that it was written on plain paper bearing the same eagle watermark.

He told me he couldn't send me a photostat of it, since Coral had asked him to keep it confidential -- though he did have the original which she had loaned him.

The most I could gather from Lex's remarks was that this letter purported to be from some Postal Department employee, who urged APRO unofficially to suspend her publication since the Government was going to "crack down" on all saucer magazines. It, too, had apparently been written on the same typewriter and mailed at or about the same time.

When I hung up I picked the receiver back up to make a local call and the operator was on the line.

"Emergency call from Mr. Moseley," she said, and, on the other end of the line, of all people, was James Moseley.

"Gray, I first want to apologize for something which isn't my fault..."

I had never before heard such a conciliatory tone in Moseley's voice,

Sent to Ted Riordan
(mid-December, 1957)

Dear Lex:

The family has been down with the flu, Linda has been having a round with the dentist, a couple had set of pirates; then I have been doing overtime. As a result everything has been disorganized and I haven't got around to answering your letter of December 4th.

We certainly have been hearing the reverberations of the November step-up in sightings, and I do think officials here are sitting up and taking notice, though you can be sure this will not come down through public channels.

Now back to another thing, I agree with you in your thoughts about allocation of funds by the Nat. Science Foundation, but as you know I am no longer connected with them and I had very little authority when I was there, as a matter of fact.

Wanda tells you hello, and that she is looking forward to "talking shop" with you again. She enjoyed the conversation very much, in fact all she could talk about was you for some time thereafter.

I do hope you can handle the matter at hand with "applomb."

Very truly yours,

"Kep"

EXHIBIT III

for as I have explained previously, we had not got along well.

"I heard part of your conversation with Mebane quite through accident. The operator was trying to cut in because I told her it was an emergency call. I suppose in some way it is, any how I have to see you immediately. I'm ready to get in my car and drive down there, can you be there?"

When he detected some reluctance in my reply he said, "Please, I think its important to you too. I've just been visited by the FBI. I think somebody is trying to frame you!"

"No kiddin!" I interjected; then the tension cooled and both of us chuckled.

"I don't want to discuss this with you over the telephone. If it's OK I'll start driving now, sleep for a few hours there in Clarksburg and see you tomorrow. Get me a room." he added.

"All right," I said, "I'll get you a room at the Waldo Hotel (which has since been purchased by a local college)."

I spent another almost sleepless night. What was it with Moseley, anyhow? Had he really written the letters and was now on the hot seat?" Was this visit some trick? Somehow I doubted it, and I looked forward to the meeting.

"Do you drink?" he asked me the next morning when he rang me up at home.

"Now and then socially," I told him but added I had nothing in the house and that the State was dry except for liquor stores.

"That's OK," he said, "there's a State store in the first floor of my hotel."

Mosely walked into my apartment, tall, gangly, just a trifle ill at ease and shy, but a handsome, clean-cut man.

"Sorry I forgot my badge," he said, "but anyhow we plain-clothes-men never wear any -- but I brought a bottle to make up for it," and he waved the paper bag. For the first time I began to get a glimpse of Moseley's great sense of humor.

"Don't you think we'd better go out for something to eat first," I suggested.

"We couldn't talk at a restaurant. You cook something and I'll talk, in the meanwhile, and that will balance the Ledger."

I poured some A&P coffee out that had just perked.

"First of all," he said, "you didn't write the Straith letter! I'll bet you are glad to know that."

"I know that too, but what makes YOU so sure?" I half kidded him.

"I had this thing pinned all over you. A special issue of SAUCER NEWS is laying in my apartment right now ready to go to press, with a big article exposing you. A letter from you printed beside the Straith letter. The whole bit, then a long article attacking your role in the affair."

"Are you threatening me?"

"I don't threaten, but I AM afraid of libel. Contrary to what you may have heard or believe, I have no income from the CIA. The fact is I'm filthy rich. I'm worth a million dollars, a few bucks more or less, depending on the daily Dow Jones averages."

I broke a cautious egg into the electric skillet and kept listening.

"I saw my lawyer to check it. He said he would have to PROVE it in case you weren't brought to trial and convicted.

"You don't know how thorough, persistent and hard-headed I am if I think I'm on to something. So I blew a few bucks -- if you only knew how many green on one of the best typewriter experts

THE STRANGE CASE OF R. E. STRAITH
in the business. He was handicapped because he was working only from a 'stat of the so-called Straith letter, but it was enough. They were written on typewriters of exactly the same typeface.

"BUT, ..." and he paused. ".... DIFFERENT TYPEWRITERS WERE INVOLVED!"

"I don't know whether to thank you or to throw you out for trying to expose me," I told Jim, "But anyhow, my mind is greatly relieved. The FBI will do a similar analysis, and they likely will come up with the same proof."

"Don't worry ..... the difference was obvious, according to the expert," he reassured me.

"On the other hand," he continued, "I might as well show you the results of some further research.....you see I've suddenly become fascinated with typewriters."

He took from his brief case a copy of a transcript of an affadavit by Dr. Daniel Norman, Director of Chemical Research in the New England Spectrochemical Laboratories, which was to be used in the retrial of Alger Hiss, who had been convicted partly on the similarity of typewriters.

"I now say to the court that Woodstock N 230099 is a Fake Machine.....it .....is a deliberately fabricated job, a new type face on an old body."

"This means then," I slowly told Jim, "that if somebody really WANTED to, they could still "prove I wrote something."

The time had come, Jim told me then, "to settle our silly feud. I don't think you seriously dislike me, and I can't imagine you really believe fantastic things you print about me either. I must say that I really admire admire your own UFO work."

Then Jim told me a great deal about himself, he was heir to a shipping fortune and had a large trust fund settled on him. His mother had died several years before, when he was a young teenager, and he had been left to live alone. His father was still living but they didn't get along. He was the son of General Van Horn Moseley an anti-Semitic who constantly wrote violent smear pamphlets and articles. The money had been inherited from his mother's side of the family.

"As to my being in the Air Force or the CIA, you know that's ridiculous. But let's carry things on as if you did believe it. Let's continue the feud in our publications, let people think we're enemies. For we're going to eventually smoke out some vermin if we work together."

Moseley had also been investigated by the FBI -- that was one of the events that brought about his decision to drive down.

I WON"T GO INTO THE THINGS THAT MOSELEY NEXT RELATED TO ME -- THEY WILL BE FOR HIM ALONE TO RELEASE IF HE EVER DARES.

In short he told me that he suspected a certain organization was behind the Straith matter, why he didn't know. This was supposed to be a civilian organization and one we both suspected. We pledged to work together secretly to try and UNCOVER further information.

As we finished our breakfast Jim told me that Lonzo Dove had just submitted an article to him with enlargements of my typing and the Straith typing, purporting to prove the type was the same.

"I don't want to tell him that I had the type analyzed by an expert and yet I can't think of a good excuse for not printing the article. I'm afraid he'll suspect that we are working together if I turn it down."

"Why don't you put it off by pointing out the possibility of libel action."

"Yes, that's what I'll do. The

article would damage you severely for many people would probably believe it."

****

Yet another letter, written in the same type size and style, was to show up. In a news letter of April 20, 1959, Laura Mundo, director of the Planetary Center, Detroit, Mich., printed a reply to a R. E. Andrews, of the United States Information Agency. Suspecting this was another "Straith" type letter, I looked into the matter and found, surely enough that she had received a similar missive, again with the familiar typeface! A careful reading of this letter did disclose a different tone from that of the the Straith letter. In our opinion (though Laura didn't interpret it in that manner it contained subtle hints that the addressed organization might be subversive: the mention of "Peace Groups," "Political Implications" and "not our policy to publicly discredit anyone.")

The investigation of this matter by Moseley and myself is still going on, though has yielded no spectacular results so far. We have concluded, for example, by blowing up signatures to large size, that the R. E. STRAITH and R. L. ANDREWS signatures were written by the same person, but that some entirely different person signed the name, "Kip". (See Exhibit No.5).

A joint conference with Jim and my attorney indicated there were no really serious problems involved

"If this report is reliable," the lawyer said, after examining the expert's report, "the same results will show up in the report the FBI will obtain."

"The Government is very careful before they prosecute a case. That's why they win so many of them. You'll likely hear no further from them."

If prosecuted, the case would be brought either on behalf of the State Department or the United States Post office.

The U. S. Code, Title 18, Section 1017, he explained, provides for a penalty of not more than $5,000.00 fine or imprisonment for not more than five years or both for "Whoever fraudently affixes or impresses the seal of any department, commission, document, or paper or with knowledge of its fraudulent character, with wrongful or fraudulent intent uses, buys, procures, sells, or transfers to another any such certificate, instrument, commission, document, or paper, to which or upon which said seal had been so fraudulently affixed or impressed."

To send such a letter through the United States mails would represent additional crime. U. S. Code, Title 18, Section 1717, declares that letters in violation of section 1017 are nommailable and shall not be conveyed in the mails or delivered from any post office or by any letter carrier. This offence carries a $5,000.00 fine and/or ten years in prison.

During a subsequent visit by FBI investigators I showed them the photostat of the letter addressed to CSI and loaned it to them. One of the men gave me a pad of paper and asked me to write the name "Kip" several times on the different sheets. A month or two later the photostat was returned to me by mail.

That was the last I ever heard from them.

While I have remained convinced that the Straith letter was indeed spurious, Richard Ogden, who did a tremendous amount of research on the Case, still believes Straith really exists.

A great deal of this research was published in the December, 1949, issue of Ray Palmer's FLYING SAUCERS magazine, of which we can report only briefly here.

We first quote Ogden on the stationery used:

"Mr Adamski's letter from the Department of State was written on a

UNITED STATES INFORMATION AGENCY
WASHINGTON

OFFICE OF
THE DIRECTOR

EXHIBIT IV

December 16th, 1957

Mrs. Laura Mundo
1014 Longfellow
Royal Oak, Mich.

My Dear Mrs. Mundo:

It has come to our attention that you are distributing and encouraging the distribution of information on the so-called "Flying Saucers" from your Michigan headquarters.

We would deeply appreciate receipt of certain information from you as follows:

(1) How many members are enrolled in your group?

(2) How many of these are dues paying members?

(3) A sample copy of your tract or tracts.

(4) Do you consider your group's study of "Flying Saucers" to have political implications?

(5) Have you received any previous official enquiries about your work?

(6) What is your personal opinion, and, also, the opinion of your group, on the so-called "peace groups"?

I do hope that someone from this department, if not myself, will soon have the pleasure of speaking with you personally, however your written reply will greatly assist us in completing our files on your group.

Any reply will be kept entirely confidential, as it is not our policy to publicly discredit anyone.

Very truly yours,

R. L. Andrews
Internal Affairs Committee
R.L.A./ob

Very truly yours,

R. L. Andrews

R. L. Andrews
Internal Affairs Commi

R. C. Strait

R. C. Strait
Cultural Exchange

Kip

EXHIBIT V

very special and highly important and restricted paper. The paper used in writing the Straith letter is known as 'white-seal, blue-embossed stationery.' This stationery is used only for the following types of correspondence of the Department of State: letters and memoranda to the President, and notes to ministers of foreign affairs, or charge d'affaires ad interim of other governments. In addition, it can be found only in Washington, D. C., in the Office of the Secretary of State under lock and key. The stationery is carefully guarded because it is used on a high governmental level. Only two persons have access to this paper: The Secretary of State and the Under Secretary. This should correct the false impression that numerous employees of the Department of State have access to the type of paper used to write the Straith letter."

Ogden as a result of his research, was convinced that there really was an R. E. Straith whose existence has deliberately been denied.

First, on March 3, 1958, he wrote a letter, marked "personal," to "Mr. R. E. Straith, Cultural Exchange Committee, Department of State, Washington 25, D. C.". Having no reply by April 5, he wrote to the office of the Secretary of State, inquiring if they had an employee by that name.

He received a prompt reply from Maurice S. Rice, Acting Chief, Public Service Division, which denied both the existence of Straith AND a Cultural Exchange Committee.

Next Ogden placed a long distance phone call to the State Department, asking for the Chairman of the Cultural Exchange Committee. The call was transferred to the office of a Mr. L.K. Little, director of personnel for the U. S. Information Agency. The office told Ogden that the Cultural Exchange Committee was part of the Cultural Presentation Staff, whose director was a James F. Magdanz. The call was next transferred to Magdanz's office. His staff, according to the U. S. Government Organization Manual, facilitied the transportation and performance of individual American artists and cultural and athletic groups overseas. When Mr. Magdanz's secretary answered the phone she would neither deny nor confirm the existence of a Cultural Exchange Committee until Ogden told her his name. As soon as she had his name she got her superior, Magdanz, on the phone, and he denied the existence of the Cultural Exchange Committee. Then, in typical Government fashion, they kept transferring the call from department to department until Ogden finally gave up in dismay.

His investigation further disclosed that the Committee was located in State Department Annex SA-20. So Ogden sent a registered letter to Straith on August 31, 1958. The delivery receipt was signed, R. E. Straith, but by another party, M. N. Hart, who had filled in Straith's name and assigned the building code, SA-20.

Ogden's many investigations finally earned for him a personal visit by the FBI which did not dismay him. He wrote to Rice about the FBI visit, and registered it, but did not receive his return receipt until a year later, when, after no reply, he complained to the Postmaster General.

Whether or not it had anything to do with his persistence in getting to the bottom of the Straith mystery and his wholehearted support of George Adamski, Ogden subsequently suffered great misfortunes. It may have no connections, and we don't want to go off on a wild tangent here. So we'll say no more of the matter at this time.

And so, the Straith letter remains one of the great unsolved mysteries of the UFO field. Due to my unpleasant experiences with it and the distrust I suffered as a result of it, I wanted to forget about it and have kept these facts to myself for nine long years.

If somebody or some agency was after ME, they have failed, for I have survived. I sincerely believe there have been other efforts to silence me, and these matters I will tell about some day. Throughout all of these persecutions, my dear friends, who have really counted, have stuck by me. In some ways I am GLAD these things happened, for I have been strengthened by the ordeals.

James Moseley and I will continue to seek out needles in haystacks, even though we may never succeed. Meanwhile we have become very close friends.

And there is the inevitable postscript to the Straith mystery. If it is authentic, it may throw additional light on the matter.

It is in the form of a letter received by Ray Palmer in late 1959:

November 10th (Enroute)

Dear Mr. Palmer:

I am dropping this letter off at the Memphis A' port. For once and for all, I want to clear up the Straith Matter. I am one of the former secretaries for the Cultural Exchange Committee. Mr. Straith's main job is collecting U.F.O. data from all the foreign countries. Only a few people know this. He is supposed to act as clearing manager for artists, musicians, etc., between countires. Your magazine is a nasty headache to the Department, as Mr. Straith is supposed to be undercover. If by chance he is found out, people are told he is retired, and lives in this country or that country.

In this department is a two foot file on you, and every letter you or your writers ever wrote are listed. There's one funny notation that said you rigged up string or wire around your place to set off a flash camera, also a notation that says, 'Burglar alarm don't work.' The metal specimens contained 'Nickel, silver, cobalt (infused) crude iron slag. The blue stuff on it is diffused copper sulphate. But back in the Committee. Ask any big singer who visited Europe about it. They may or may not talk. I am trying to disguise this handwriting in case you photostat this letter and publish it. I would lose my present position if some person recognized it.

I wish I could clear up the mess (which I can) but I am afraid to do so......Wish I could tell you more, but can't.

(signed) Well wisher.

P.S. There are no finger prints on this letter.

Made in the USA
San Bernardino, CA
27 July 2015